Quality Matters in Children's Services

Quality Matters in Children's Services

Series Editor: Mike Stein
Consultant Editor: Caroline Thomas

The provision of high quality Children's Services matters to those who use and provide Children's Services. This important series is the result of an extensive government-funded research initiative into the *Quality Protects* programme which aimed to improve outcomes for vulnerable children, as well as transform the management and delivery of Children's Services. Focussing on current challenges in making every child matter, titles in the series are essential reading for all those working in the field.

Mike Stein is a research professor in the Social Policy Research Unit at the University of York. He has researched the problems and challenges faced by vulnerable children and young people for 25 years and contributed to the development of policy and practice in the UK and internationally. He acted as an academic adviser to the *Quality Protects* research initiative. Caroline Thomas is Senior Research Fellow at the Department of Applied Social Science, University of Stirling, UK. She is an academic adviser to the Department for Children, Schools and Families.

other books in the series

Child Protection, Domestic Violence and Parental Substance Misuse
Family Experiences and Effective Practice
Hedy Cleaver, Don Nicholson, Sukey Tarr and Deborah Cleaver
ISBN 978 1 84310 582 4

Educating Difficult Adolescents
Effective Education for Children in Public Care or with Emotional and Behavioural Difficulties
David Berridge, Cherilyn Dance, Jennifer Beecham and Sarah Field
ISBN 978 1 84310 681 4

Kinship Care
Fostering Effective Family and Friends Placements
Elaine Farmer and Sue Moyers
ISBN 978 1 84310 631 9

The Pursuit of Permanence
A Study of the English Child Care System
Ian Sinclair, Claire Baker, Jenny Lee and Ian Gibbs
ISBN 978 1 84310 595 4

Quality
Matters
in **Children's**
Services

Quality Matters in **Children's Services**

Messages from Research

▶ Mike Stein
▶ Foreword by Baroness Delyth Morgan,
Parliamentary Undersecretary of State for
Children, Young People and Families

Jessica Kingsley Publishers
London and Philadelphia

First published in 2009
by Jessica Kingsley Publishers
116 Pentonville Road
London N1 9JB, UK
and
400 Market Street, Suite 400
Philadelphia, PA 19106, USA

www.jkp.com

Library of Congress Cataloging in Publication Data

Stein, Mike.
  Quality matters in children's services : messages from research / Mike Stein.
     p. cm.
  Includes bibliographical references and index.
  ISBN 978-1-84310-926-6 (pb : alk. paper) 1. Children--Services for. 2. Child welfare. 3.
Quality assurance. I. Title.
  HV713.S83 2009
  362.7'30684--dc22
                                                           2008045120

British Library Cataloguing in Publication Data
A CIP catalogue record for this book is available from the British Library

ISBN 978 1 84310 926 6

Printed and bound in Great Britain by
Printwise (Haverhill) Ltd, Suffolk

Contents

List of Figures

Acknowledgements

Many people have contributed along the journey to bring about this Overview.

Caroline Thomas, who jointly co-ordinated the *Quality Protects* research initiative was there at the start, when we selected the research projects, and has been a source of ongoing support, advice and wisdom.

Caroline also skilfully chaired the Advisory and Implementation Group (AIG) which was led with enthusiasm and commitment by Celia Atherton and Jo Tunnard. The membership of the AIG (see Appendix B), drawn from Children's Services, made an important contribution in drawing out the policy and practice implications from the research studies, and in identifying the key questions for senior staff, managers and practitioners.

The core content of the Overview is derived from the research studies, although it can only do justice to a small part of the work undertaken by the researchers. I am indebted to them for their time, skill and expertise, and hope that I have done justice in the selection and interpretation of their work.

Finally, as any researcher worth their salt will tell you, their work would not be possible without the co-operation of those who provide and use the services they are researching. To those who work in Children's Services, and the parents, children and young people, whose own lives have not been easy, but who give of their time freely, a big thank you.

The epigraph quotes in Chapters 2–7 are taken from the research studies.

Foreword

In the last 10 years we have witnessed a quiet revolution in the way services and professionals support and protect looked after children and other children in need. From Quality Protects in 1998, to *Care Matters* and the recent *Children's Plan*, our vision has put children at the centre of a system designed to nurture them, linked by the golden thread of the Every Child Matters framework. We recognise the part that everyone plays, helping the most vulnerable children to be happy and healthy, enjoying their childhood, achieving their potential, and preparing for their future. We also acknowledge the Government's important leadership role, helping those who work most closely with children and young people to be ambitious for those in their care, excellent in their practice, committed to partnership, and respected and valued as professionals.

Good quality research and evidence is a crucial element of effective and consistent practice, and the purpose of the nine studies featured in this volume is to share successes and experience widely, to encourage innovation and excellence. We commissioned these studies to examine the impact of *Quality Protects* on the quality of services for children in care, those in the child protection system, and other children who needed support from Children's Services.

This overview covers a valuable range of topics which are pertinent to the future quality of services and outcomes for the children and families they serve. These include placement stability and children's wellbeing; the education of vulnerable young people; child protection, domestic violence and parental substance misuse; and, crucially, the participation of children and young people themselves. We have also taken this opportunity to showcase effective structural and systemic reform in practice, including the stakeholder engagement; integrated working; developing organisational processes; conducting assessments; and training and workforce reform.

It is clear from what follows that progress has been made but that we cannot allow ourselves to be complacent. The story it tells will not surprise us, but reinforces the importance of our commitments in *Care Matters: Time for Change* and the Children and Young Persons Act 2008. The quality of a placement and that of the child's relationship with their carer is by far the most important influence on a child's wellbeing, and social workers play a pivotal part. To support this we need to capture, record and evaluate information about children who enter and leave care, and using this to inform and shape policies and services, to make sure this is the best country in the world for *every* child to grow up, whatever their circumstances, wherever they are.

All those working with the most vulnerable children and their families can be proud of what has been achieved so far, and hopefully use these findings to further develop good practice and excellent services. Working with you, we will continue to celebrate and build on your success.

Baroness Delyth Morgan,
Parliamentary Undersecretary of State for Children,
Young People and Families

The Overview Process

Background

The *Messages from Research* overviews and the process for their development have their origins in the 1980s. The first in the series was written by Jane Rowe. This brought together the findings from nine Department of Health-funded studies and had decision-making as its clear, central and unifying theme. This overview's overall aim was to help social workers to absorb and make use of the findings. The overview, *Social Work Decisions in Child Care*, often referred to within the social work profession as 'The Pink Book', received a warm welcome and laid a firm foundation for the *Messages from Research* series. Nine overviews have subsequently been published.

Reflecting on her experiences of writing two of the early overviews, Jane Rowe wrote of the invaluable 'insights, ideas and collective wisdom' of her Advisory Groups of researchers, social work practitioners and policy-makers. Over the years the tradition of having an Advisory Group to support the development of the overviews has been well maintained. However, the remit of these groups has been extended beyond the production of the overview to include consideration of the wider dissemination of the research and its implementation into professional practice. The groups now aim to make the overviews and the findings within them accessible and relevant to a wide range of stakeholders. Membership has widened to reflect the range of professionals and agencies now providing services to children and their families in England, and the new organisational arrangements for their delivery. It has also broadened to include specialists in the dissemination of research and training.

Current Overview – Quality Matters in Children's Services: Messages from Research

Members of the Advisory and Implementation Group for *Quality Matters in Children's Services: Messages from Research* included representatives from local authority Children's Services departments, health and education professionals, Ofsted, national organisations concerned with child welfare, researchers and Department for Children, Schools and Families (DCSF) policy advisers. The work of the group was led by the research dissemination and implementation organisation, Research in Practice.

At least two members read each of the nine studies, summarised the key findings and assessed their main implications for professional practice. Members also developed from the findings strategic, operational and practice questions relating to the quality of Children's Services. These questions are addressed to commissioners, managers and practitioners of Children's Services. Mike Stein, Research Professor at the Social Policy Research Unit at the University of York, and co-ordinator of the *Quality Protects* research initiative, took responsibility for authorship of the text. He did so on the basis of the members' presentations and discussions of this material, and his own reading and careful analysis of the reports. The researchers who had undertaken the studies contributed short written summaries of their work to be incorporated into the overview as an appendix[1]. Drafts of the full overview were reviewed and discussed by the Group. Finally, Mike Stein took responsibility for finalising the text.

The Group recognised that the overview report itself is unlikely to reach all those with an interest in its messages. Members therefore advised on, and became involved in, the production of other dissemination and implementation materials, some of which are targeted at specific professional or service-user groups. These materials include film, video, pod-casts, e-learning and leaflets. Information about the full range of these materials is available on the Department for Children, Schools and Families *Every Child Matters* website: www.ecm.gov.uk/qualitymatters, accessed 3 November 2008.

Chapter 1

Quality Matters

> What if this was my child? Would it be good enough for them?
>
> (John Hutton, then Minister of State for Social Services, 1998)

What's in a name?

Why Quality?

The title of this book, *Quality Matters in Children's Services: Messages from Research*, requires some explanation. It has a heritage derived from both policy and research.

Why *Quality*? Quality, as well as denoting a high degree of excellence, an aspiration shared by those who provide and use Children's Services, also has a more specific lineage, the *Quality Protects* programme. This was launched by the Department of Health in September 1998 – originally as a three-year programme but extended to five years – with the main aim of improving outcomes for children and young people who were in need, and in particular those looked after by local authorities. The revelations of widespread abuse in children's homes, as well as research evidence showing poor educational and career outcomes for many children and young people whilst living in and leaving care, provided the catalyst for change: more than 75 per cent of care leavers had no academic qualifications of any kind and over half of young people leaving care after 16 were unemployed.

In his 'launch' letter to councillors on 21 September 1998, the then Secretary of State, Frank Dobson, highlighted the responsibility of local government in 'delivering high quality services', and the 'legal and moral duty to provide the kind of loyal support that any good parent would give to their children'. In similar vein, in addressing councillors, as 'corporate parents', John Hutton, his then Minister of State for Social Services, commented: 'We are determined that *Quality Protects* will change the system. You need to be asking yourself, what if this was my child? Would it be good enough for them? Would it be good enough for me?'

The *Quality Protects* programme aimed to support local authorities in transforming their Children's Services. There were four main elements:

- Eleven defined national objectives, with linked sub-objectives and performance indicators.
- Management Action Plans and progress reports.
- A key role for councillors, acting as 'corporate parents', in delivering the programme.
- A five-year Children's Services special grant.

Payment of the special grant was dependent on local authorities identifying service deficiencies and having clear proposals to overcome these within their Management Action Plans. Funding was to be targeted on improvements in specific service areas: the supply of adoptive, foster and residential placements; support for young people leaving care; services for disabled children; listening to the views of children and young people; assessment, planning and record keeping; and management information and quality assurance systems.

The *Quality Protects* programme also provided the dynamic for the *Guidance on the Education of Children and Young People in Public Care* published in 2000, as well as the setting up of the *Quality Protects* Health Group, and the issuing of the Guidance, *Promoting the Health of Looked After Children*, in 2002. The Guidance in these two areas provided stepping stones to future policy developments in education and health, the former detailed in Chapter 6, *Caring and Educating*, the latter including the *National Healthy Care Standard and Handbook* (2005), and Healthy Care partnerships, aimed at improving the health of looked after children and young people through multi-agency partnerships.

The introduction of the Children (Leaving Care) Act 2000 (in October 2001) was a response to the plight of care leavers, targeted by Objective 5 of *Quality Protects*: '*to ensure that young people leaving care, as they enter adulthood, are not isolated and participate socially and economically as citizens*'. This led to the 1999 consultation document, *Me, Survive, Out There?* which set out the main proposals for legislative change.

Quality Protects was also part of a wider set of policy initiatives to combat social exclusion. This included Sure Start and the Children's Fund which aimed to help younger children and their families in disadvantaged areas, and the introduction of the Connexions service, to support young people during their journey into post-16 education, employment and training. The Youth Justice Board was established in 1998, and at the local level, since 2000, multi-agency 'youth offending teams' have been introduced in England and Wales. Their 'statutory' membership includes Children's Services (children's social care and education), health, probation and police. There have also been wider initiatives to tackle youth homelessness, under-achievement in education, teenage parenthood and neighbourhood renewal.

Why Matters?

Returning to the overview title, why *Matters*? As well as Children's Services *mattering* – being of vital importance to those who use them – *Matters*, also has a policy lineage. The seeds were sown by *Quality Protects*, in the expectation that '*all children gain maximum life chances*'. Their lives matter. *Choice Protects*, introduced in March 2002, also reflected the focus on outcomes, with its aim to improve stability and choice in foster care placements.

Building on these policy developments, the Government published their Green Paper, *Every Child Matters* in 2003. It identified four key themes:

- Increasing the focus on supporting parents and carers.
- Early intervention and effective protection.
- Strengthening accountability and the integration of services at all levels.
- Workforce reform.

The Government's aim for all children and young people, whatever their background or circumstances, was to have the support they need to improve outcomes in five key areas: being healthy; staying safe; enjoying and achieving; making a positive contribution; and achieving economic well-being. Published alongside the Government's response to the report into the death of Victoria Climbié, *Every Child Matters* resulted in a major consultation exercise and review of Children's Services.

This led to the publication of *Every Child Matters: The Next Steps* and the Children Act 2004, the latter strengthening the legal framework to protect and safeguard children from harm. The *National Service Framework for Children, Young People and Maternity Services*, also published in 2004, set out a ten-year programme to stimulate long-term and sustained improvement in children's health and well-being. In November 2004, *Every Child Matters: Change for Children* identified new ways in which all organisations involved with children and young people could work better together.

But that was not the end of what *Matters* in policy. In 2005, *Youth Matters* set out the Government's priorities to support young people outside of schools, including action to give young people more say in how their needs are met. In October 2006, the Government published their Green Paper, *Care Matters: Transforming the Lives of Children and Young People in Care*, against the background of continuing evidence of poor educational and career outcomes for looked after children. In March and May 2007, *Aiming High for Children: Supporting Families* and *Aiming High for Disabled Children: Better Support for Families*, detailed proposals and services to families, for improving outcomes for vulnerable and disabled children and young people.

The wide range of responses to the *Care Matters* consultation document contributed to the White Paper, *Care Matters: Time for Change*, published in June 2007, whose main proposals constituted the Children and Young Persons Act 2008. Also, in response to the recommendations of the *Review of the Child Care Proceedings System in England and Wales*, published in 2006, revised statutory Guidance (The Children Act 1989 Guidance and Regulations, Volume 1, Court Orders, 2008), and a new Public Law Outline has been introduced, from April 2008. These changes are aimed to reduce the impact of delay on children and young people involved in child care proceedings, as the longer it takes to make a decision, the longer children and young people have to wait for permanence, and thus the more likely they are to be 'coming and going' (Chapter 2).

In December 2007, the Department for Children, Schools and Families published *The Children's Plan: Building Brighter Futures*, setting out goals for improving the well-being and health, safety, education and careers, of children and young people, by 2020. This included a commitment to a *Staying Safe: Action Plan*, published in 2008, covering the full span of the *Every Child Matters* 'staying safe' outcome with proposals organised to cover *universal* (all children and young people), *targeted* (vulnerable groups of children and young people) and *responsive* (children and young people who have been harmed) safety issues. Also linked to the Children's Plan was the issuing of statutory Guidance on Children's Trusts – entrusted with responsibility of delivering the 'high ambitions' of the Children's Plan, in placing the family 'at the centre of excellent integrated services'.

In March 2008, the implementation plan, *Care Matters: Time to Deliver for Children in Care* was launched to drive the national improvement plan for looked after children. Like *Quality Protects*, ten years earlier, it highlighted the poor outcomes of looked after children and those leaving care, recognising that although there had been some progress, as well as differences between the performance of local authorities, overall, a lot still remained to be done. In responding to the 'depth of the challenge', the *Care Matters* implementation plan also echoed the main themes arising from the wide range of policy developments outlined in Figure 1.1.

- Combating social exclusion.
- Universal aspirations and improving outcomes for vulnerable children and young people and their families.
- Multi-agency partnerships and integrated working.
- Personalisation of services.
- Early intervention and family support.
- 'Excellent' corporate parenting.
- Empowering service users.

Figure 1.1 Policy framework for the development of quality services

These themes can be seen as providing the policy framework for the development of quality Children's Services. They will be revisited in the subsequent chapters, along with the policy initiatives described above, and other policy developments relevant to the specific studies, in order to provide a contemporary context for the research reviewed in the Overview.

Why Children's Services?

The inclusion of *Children's Services* in the Overview title also has a lineage in law and policy. As detailed below (in the discussion of 'Who is the Overview aimed at'), given the origins, aims and focus of the *Quality Protects* programme and research initiative, the Overview title could have been *Quality Matters in Children's Social Care*. It certainly would have been simpler, but at the same time this title would have ignored the changing legal, policy and practice context.

First, since the introduction of the Children Act 2004 local authorities have combined their children's social care and education functions under a new Director of Children's Services, and also have a designated lead member for Children's Services. Second, in response to the *Every Child Matters* agenda and the Children's Plan, local authorities are in the process of moving their focus from structures to outcomes and, as part of that process, including all agencies that are involved in improving outcomes for children and young people – as reflected in the membership of Children's Trusts, Local Safeguarding Children Boards, Healthy Care Partnerships and Multi-Agency Looked-After Partnerships. As detailed above, in addition to children's social care and education, this may include health, housing, probation, police and third sector organisations.

Third, the *Common Assessment Framework* is also a key practice component in the implementation of *Every Child Matters*. It sets out a framework to be used by all Children's Services – multi-disciplinary teams – to improve co-operation and information sharing, for children with additional needs, in contributing to effective early intervention. The introduction of the *Integrated Children's System* aims to provide an effective electronic case management system for documenting progress of children in need.

It is also intended that the *Common Core of Skills and Knowledge* linked to the *Children's Workforce Strategy* will improve shared understanding through a curriculum covered by all those working in Children's Services.

Why Messages from Research?

Finally, *Messages from Research*, or the '*implications*' of research findings, has featured in the title of most of the research overviews since the first 'Pink Book', *Social Work Decisions in Child Care, Recent Research Findings and their Implications*, was published in 1985. The intention has been to capture the essence of the research studies that are relevant to policy-makers, service providers and busy practitioners.

What are the research studies?

Running alongside the *Quality Protects* programme has been the research initiative. Its overall aim has been to examine the impact of the programme on the quality of services for children and young people, in respect of five of the 11 *QP* objectives – in that sense, the initiative is distinct from the programme.

Two sets of studies are included in this overview. First, those commissioned under the *Quality Protects* research initiative. In exploring the impact of *Quality Protects*, they have examined how the objectives of the programme are being translated into practice. This includes an evaluation of some of the changes in policy, procedure and practice introduced in response to the programme, and an assessment of outcomes for children, young people and their families in relation to their welfare and quality of life. Second, also included, are selected studies funded by the Department of Health which have informed the development of *Quality Protects* and have also contributed to its ongoing evaluation. The studies included in the Overview were carried out at different times, between 2001 and 2007, including the fieldwork, analysis and write-up of the findings.

Summaries of all these studies, including their research design, samples and conclusions are presented later (see Appendix A). The present chapter identifies the studies and provides a brief outline. The studies are grouped together under five of the main objectives of the *Quality Protects* programme.

Objective 1: To ensure that children are securely attached to carers capable of providing safe and effective care for the duration of childhood – by ensuring more stability.

- *The Pursuit of Permanence: A Study of the English Care System* (Ian Sinclair, Clare Baker, Jenny Lee and Ian Gibbs, University of York).

  This was a large-scale quantitative and qualitative study of 7399 looked after children in 13 councils. It focused on all children looked after in the course of a year the last day which fell between 31 May 2003 and 30 June 2004. It covered their full placement careers, changes of legal status, reasons for admission, age at first entry to care, types of placement and dates on which placements started and ended. Data was also collected from social workers, team leaders, senior managers, and case studies based on interviews with young people and their social workers. National data was used to contextualise the research, including the use of performance indicators.

- *The Reunification of Looked After Children with their Parents: Patterns, Interventions and Outcomes* (Elaine Farmer, Wendy Sturgess and Teresa O'Neill, University of Bristol).

This study examined the patterns and outcomes of return home by means of a two-year follow-up of a sample of 180 looked after children who were returned to their parents between January and December 2001. It describes the experiences of children prior to, during and after their return home and identifies the factors associated with successful and unsuccessful returns. The sample was drawn from six local authorities and the data sources included case file reviews and interviews with parents, children and their social workers.

- *Support Foster Care: Developing a Short-Break Service for Children in Need* (Margaret Greenfields and June Statham, Thomas Coram Research Unit, University of London).

  This study investigated the extent to which local authorities in England were developing 'support care' schemes to provide short breaks with another carer for children at times of particular difficulty or stress, combined with support for their parents. It aimed to identify the barriers deterring local authorities from providing this kind of support and how they might be overcome. Data sources included a questionnaire sent to all English local authorities (46 councils responded), telephone interviews and an in-depth study of selected schemes (14 schemes). The fieldwork was carried out between March and August 2003.

- *Kinship Care: Fostering Effective Family and Friends Placements* (Elaine Farmer and Sue Moyers, University of Bristol).

  This study examined the characteristics, progress and outcomes of children placed with family and friends, compared these with a similar group of children placed with unrelated foster carers, and considered the factors that contribute to success in kin placements. It is based upon case file reviews (270), half of which related to children living with family or friends and half with unrelated foster carers, on a set date (July 2000) and followed-up for two years. There were also in-depth interviews with 32 kin carers and with children, social workers and parents.

- *Keeping Them in the Family: Outcomes for Children Placed in Kinship Care Through Care Proceedings* (Joan Hunt, Suzette Waterhouse and Eleanor Lutman, University of Oxford).

  This study has explored the outcomes for children placed with members of their extended families or social networks, as a result of care proceedings, following child protection concerns. It is based on a sample of 113 children placed with family and friends and 31 children placed with unrelated carers, followed up during 2004 and 2005. Data sources include case files (144) and interviews with carers (37), children and young people (14), parents (2) and social workers (24). In addition, measurements of child functioning and carer well-being were carried out.

Objective 2: To ensure that children are protected from emotional, physical and sexual abuse, and neglect.

- *Child Protection, Domestic Violence and Parental Substance Misuse, Family Experiences and Effective Practice* (Hedy Cleaver, Don Nicholson, Sukey Tarr and Deborah Cleaver, Royal Holloway, University of London).

   The focus of this study is children referred to children's social care where there are safeguarding concerns and evidence of domestic violence and/or, parental substance abuse within families. The study, carried out between 2002 and 2005, was based in six local authorities and involved an analysis of agency plans, procedures and protocols, questionnaires from managers and training officers (78), a study of case files (357), and interviews with parents and professionals (17).

Objective 4: To ensure that children looked after gain maximum life chance benefits from educational opportunities, health care and social care.

- *Educating Difficult Adolescents: Effective Education for Children in Public Care or with Emotional and Behavioural Difficulties* (David Berridge, University of Bristol, Cherilyn Dance, University of Bedfordshire, Jennifer Beecham, University of Kent, and Sarah Field, University of Bedfordshire).

   This study, carried out between 2003 and 2006, investigated the care, educational experiences and outcomes of adolescent pupils presenting behavioural difficulties. The study followed-up a sample of young people (150), equally divided between groups living in foster homes, children's homes and residential special schools for pupils presenting 'behavioural, emotional and social difficulties'. Also, the costs of care, educational and other professional services provided were analysed and linked to outcomes.

Objective 6: To ensure that children with specific social needs arising out of a disability or a health condition are living in settings where their assessed needs can be met.

Objective 8: To actively involve users and carers in planning services and in tailoring individual packages of care: and to ensure effective mechanisms are in place to handle complaints – by: actively involving children and families in planning and reviewing the services they use, and the decisions which affect them; and by ensuring that children in care have trusted people to whom they can speak and who will speak on their behalf to local authorities and others.

- *Participation of Disabled Children and Young People Under Quality Protects* (Anita Franklinr and Patricia Sloper, University of York).

    This study carried out between 2003 and 2005 has investigated the processes and outcomes of disabled children's participation in decision-making. It includes children and young people with complex health needs; autistic spectrum disorders; communication impairments and degenerative conditions. Data sources included an analysis of Management Action Plans, a survey of all English local authorities (71 responses), qualitative methods with children and young people (21), parents (24) and staff (76) in selected local authorities.

- *Advocacy for Looked After Children and Children in Need* (Christine Oliver, Abigail Knight and Mano Candappa, Thomas Coram Research Unit, University of London).

    This study, carried out between 2003 and 2005, has explored the role of advocacy in facilitating the participation of looked after children, and children in need, in decision-making. Data sources have included a literature review, a telephone survey of advocacy services in England (75 responses), and a qualitative study of selected advocacy services based on interviews with children and young people (48), advocates (18), parents and carers (13) and professionals (40).

What ideas have informed the overview?

The *Quality Protects* initiative and the research studies included in this overview have been influenced by, draw on, and develop some key concepts and ideas. This includes social exclusion, attachment theory, safeguarding, participation, and parenting. These are briefly outlined below, linked to the research studies, and further discussed in the relevant chapters in the overview. As a health warning, it is not suggested that they are exhaustive, nor are they necessarily mutually exclusive. In addition, I have suggested that *resilience* which has not explicitly informed the Overview may be of particular relevance to the group of children and young people who were the focus of the initiative.

Social exclusion

At the policy level, as discussed above, *Quality Protects* was one of a series of Government initiatives designed to combat the *social exclusion* of vulnerable children and young people. The programme's prime objective of improving outcomes for children and young people in need, and in particular those looked after by local authorities, was in recognition of evidence of their high risk of exclusion. They often come from the most disadvantaged social groups – parental poverty, family breakdown, maltreatment, lack of family and social support networks, and high levels of special educational needs, often casting a long shadow on their future education, health and well-being: being in care is one of the most important predictors of social exclusion in adulthood. Social exclusion has come to mean both material disadvantage and marginalisation. Whereas the former is usually associated with low income and relative poverty, the latter refers to the way groups may be excluded, omitted or stigmatised by the majority due to characteristics such as gender, age, ethnicity, disability or behaviour. Also, these two meanings are often linked, merging causes and outcomes – such as unemployment and social isolation.

In response to the evidence of exclusion on both these dimensions, the *Quality Protects* programme, and subsequent policy developments leading to the *Every Child Matters* agenda identifies looked after children and young people as having complex needs, those who require targeted and specialist support in order to both achieve good developmental outcomes for each child as set out in the *Assessment Framework* and the five Every Child Matters population outcomes. But also within an 'exclusion' perspective there is recognition that specific groups of looked after children and those in need may face additional disadvantages, including those with emotional and behavioural difficulties, disabled children, and minority ethnic children and young people. *Educating Difficult Adolescents*, discussed in Chapter 6, is included under Objective 4, of the programme and the *Participation* study, included under Objective 6 and 8 of the programme, focuses on '*children with specific social needs arising out of a disability or a health condition.*'

Attachment theory, quality of care and well-being

At the child care practice level, Objective 1 of the programme – '*to ensure that children are securely attached*' is derived from attachment theory – recognition of the influence of this perspective in understanding the lives of looked after children. Research work on attachment and loss has documented the impact of actual or threatened separation on young children and patterns of behaviour produced by unsatisfactory interaction with parents. Research has also explored how disturbances in attachment are reflected in the way a child sees the world and processes information – via an internal working model – and how these processes may lead to enduring maladaptive styles of relationships and behaviours in childhood, adolescence and adulthood.

Within the wider context of social exclusion, and recognition of cultural diversity – and these are significant influences – attachment theory provides a framework for exploring the separation of children from their families and the circumstances surrounding it, their care careers, including placement disruption or stability, and the legacy of these experiences for their lives in and after care. The five studies included under Objective 1 are concerned with the *pursuit*, or provision of permanence or stability (Chapter 2), by returning children home, or maintaining them at home through support foster care (Chapter 3), or placing them with kinship carers (Chapter 4) – or providing a compensatory attachment and a 'secure base' – for children and young people who, for whatever reason, are initially separated from their families.

However, there has been a tendency in recent child care policy and practice to view 'stability' as synonymous with 'attachment', perhaps not surprising given the research evidence that children and young people who experience multiple moves often have very poor outcomes, and become increasingly unable to use the relationships offered by carers. But neither should children remain in damaging or poor quality placements – as those who lingered in children's homes where they were being abused over many years can testify. It is the *quality of care* and its contribution to *child well-being* that matters. Both these concepts, as well as underpinning the five studies grouped under Objective 1, are also explored in the *Educating Difficult Adolescents* study included in Objective 4, '*to ensure that children looked after gain maximum life chance benefits from educational opportunities, health care and social care*' and revisited in the concluding chapter.

Safeguarding

The idea of *safeguarding* is central to Objective 2 of the *Quality Protects* programme '*to ensure that children are protected from emotional, physical and sexual abuse, and neglect.*' *Working Together to Safeguard Children* (2006), one of the key documents detailing *Every Child Matters* policy and practice, describes 'safeguarding and promoting the welfare of children' as: protecting children from maltreatment; preventing impairment of children's health and development; ensuring that children are growing up in circumstances consistent with the provision of safe and effective care; and undertaking that role so as to enable these children to have optimum life chances and to enter adulthood successfully.

This description makes it clear that 'safeguarding' is much wider in scope than protecting children, embracing both prevention and promotion. *Working Together to Safeguard Children* details how 'child protection' relates to 'safeguarding'.

'Child protection is a part of safeguarding and promoting welfare. This refers to the activity which is undertaken to protect specific children who are suffering or are at risk of suffering significant harm.'

In addition to the specific *Child Protection* study (Chapter 5), included under Objective 2, different dimensions of safeguarding are also explored in the other Overview studies.

Participation

As detailed in Chapter 7, the participation of children and young people in decision-making has become a central platform of Government policy, as a result of major shifts in law, policy, theory and practice. Nowhere is this more evident than in relation to looked after children and young people. The *Quality Protects* programme was therefore able to draw upon a body of existing work, whilst at the same time recognising that there were considerable variations in participation practice between local authorities, and in respect of different groups of children and young people. In addition, developing *effective* participation was an ongoing challenge.

In this context, Objective 8 of *Quality Protects* proposes '*actively involving children and families in planning and reviewing the services they use, and the decisions which affect them*', and '*ensuring that children in care have trusted people to whom they can speak and who will speak on their behalf to local authorities and others*'. Also, one of the targeted service areas identified for funding within the programme is 'listening to the views of children and young people'. *The Participation* and *Advocacy* studies (Chapter 7) specifically explore different dimensions of participation, including the participation of disabled children, and advocacy for looked after children. It is also a reflection of the priority afforded to participation that the views of children and young people are sought in most of the other studies discussed in this Overview.

Parenting

A body of research shows that the quality of parenting is closely associated with children and young people achieving the *Every Child Matters* outcomes, as well as reducing social exclusion, enhancing their well-being, ensuring their safety, encouraging their participation and promoting their resilience – the areas discussed above. It is also recognised that a wide range of influences impact upon parents, and how they care for their children, including social and economic policies, formal and informal support, the quality of relationships with partners, relatives and friends, and their own experience of being parented. As highlighted in an earlier Overview, *Supporting Parents: Messages from Research* (2004), we now take it for granted that parenting has to be seen in an ecological context.

The purpose of care is to ensure that children are attached to carers capable of providing safe and effective care for the duration of childhood. Whilst the appropriate pathway to permanence is being developed, children and young people need good quality social and psychological parenting from their carers. There are a number of strands to current family and parenting policy that are very relevant to the studies in this Overview, and are discussed in subsequent chapters. First, recognition of the complex needs of families who face a large number of problems and are deeply disadvantaged – it is their children who are at a high risk of coming into care. Second, recognition of the need for a continuum of support services for parents. Third, responding to the needs of the whole family, not just the parents or children and young people in isolation, in particular through planned integrated working. Fourth, for those children and young people who come in to care, the provision of high quality corporate parenting.

Resilience

The focus of recent policy developments on vulnerable children and young people highlights the potential of *resilience* as a theoretical construct – although not specifically identified in either the *Quality Protects* objectives or the *Every Child Matters* five universal outcomes. Resilience can be defined as the quality that enables some young people to find fulfilment in their lives despite their disadvantaged backgrounds, the problems or adversity they may have undergone or the pressures they may experience. Resilience is about overcoming the odds, coping and recovery. Promoting the resilience of children and young people in need, and those looked after by local authorities, by identifying risk and protective factors, including what services, policies and practices contribute to good outcomes, and translating these research messages into the development of quality services, is central to this overview.

What is the scope and limitations of this Overview?

This Overview differs from many of the earlier ones. It doesn't, for example, focus upon a specific form of care, such as foster or residential care. Neither is it dedicated to a specific activity such as child protection or parenting support. As is evident from the discussion so far, and the brief outline of the studies presented above, it is derived from the wide ranging national objectives of the *Quality Protects* programme. The nine studies included in this Overview are related, in the main, to five of the 11 national objectives. In this respect, the overview is not an exhaustive account of the range of national objectives identified in the *Quality Protects* programme. Nevertheless, the selected studies cover a wide range of topics that are pertinent to the development of quality Children's Services.

In each of these areas there is an existing body of literature, including both empirical and theoretical work. Some of this work will be referred to (referencing will be indicative), as suggested above, in order to provide a context for the selected studies and specific arguments. But this will be selective, and consistent with the rationale of the Overview – to draw out the messages of research for policy and practice.

Also, as is clear from the research outlines, the different designs of the core studies result in different sources of evidence. Taken together, this includes: descriptive data – such as personal characteristics of different respondents derived from questionnaires; the views of children and young people, parents and carers, and a range of professional staff, gathered by interviews, questionnaires, focus groups or case records; and the evaluation of outcomes, using instruments, schedules and statistical techniques. But sense has to be made of all this data through quantitative and qualitative analysis, and ultimately, by the judgements of the researchers. As other Overview authors have pointed out, all these sources have their weaknesses, as well as their strengths. But by making their research design and methodology clear, and identifying the limitations of their studies – for example in sample size, response rates, or whether the study design is descriptive or evaluative – the reader is in a position to make their own judgement on the conclusions.

Who is the Overview aimed at?

The main target group of earlier research Overviews has, in the main, been practitioners and managers in children's social work. And at first sight it would seem, for three reasons, that the present Overview should be aimed at a similar group: first, given the aims of the *Quality Protects* programme in improving outcomes for 'children in need, and those looked after by local authorities'; second, given the lead role of children's social care in delivering these services; and third, given the foci of the studies commissioned under the research initiative.

But as detailed above, the child care policy and practice world has changed since the beginning of the *Quality Protects* programme – a change, in part initiated by the *QP* programme through the introduction of 'corporate parenting'. Today, *Every Child Matters* to everyone. This is reflected in the changing organisational structures in Children's Services, including membership of Children's Trusts, the Local Safeguarding Children Boards, Healthy Care Partnerships and Multi-Agency Looked After Partnerships, as well as in key practice processes, such as the *Common Assessment Framework* (2006).

Another significant change is that the boundaries between different occupational groups in Children's Services – or professional identities – are becoming more permeable. For example, a children's social worker, a school counsellor, a mental health worker from a Child and Adolescent Mental Health team, or a worker from a youth offending team, may work with children and young people with similar needs. There are also changes in the way services are provided, including service commissioning.

In this context, although the substantive findings from the research studies are primarily concerned with children's social care, as was the intention at the time they were commissioned and carried out, the studies also raise issues for practitioners, managers and commissioners in Children's Services, more widely, including education and health services, that impact upon the well-being of very vulnerable children and young people. These issues, and in particular those related to multi-disciplinary working are identified in each chapter as 'Integrated working: issues arising from research' (Figures 2.2, 3.1, 4.1, 5.1, 6.2 and 7.1), and in the conclusions and 'Questions for Children's Services', at the end of each chapter. This is done within the parameters of the *Quality Protects* research initiative, and the *QP* objectives under which the studies were commissioned, as identified above.

How is the Overview organised?

Each of the individual chapters is organised in a broadly similar way. First, the topic will be introduced by summarising some of the key issues from earlier literature, as well as recent policy developments. Second, the main findings from the studies will be outlined. This will include brief examples of 'promoting quality' based on an individual case, organisational change or policy and practice initiative. Third, their implications for policy and practice will be summarised, including 'Integrated working: issues arising from research'. Finally, each chapter identifies 'Questions for Children's Services'. These have been prepared in discussion with members of the Implementation and Advisory Group (Appendix B) and aim to provide the reader with an opportunity to reflect on the issues raised by the studies, and, in particular think about their relevance to improving the quality of their Children's Services. The 'questions' are identified at three levels: the *strategic level*, including those responsible for directing and commissioning services; the *operational level*, including senior managers and heads of services; and the *practice level*, including front-line Children's Services staff and their managers. If these are recognised as 'three levels of quality', then a comprehensive approach to improving quality in Children's Services suggests that action will be required at all three levels, as well as consistency between them.

The chapters which follow are arranged to reflect the key themes of the *Quality Protects* objectives.

The first theme is 'attachment, stability and well-being', and the studies discussed in Chapters 2, 3 and 4 explore different dimensions. Chapter 2, *Coming and Going*, however, does more than that. It also sets the scene for the Overview by presenting a nationally representative picture of how the care system works in what the researchers call *the pursuit of permanence*. Its description includes the different purposes of care, as well as the different groups of children and young people and their pathways through care. It is these pathways that are the subject of the other Overview studies. Chapter 3, *Going Home*, explores the experiences of children returning home, and children having short-term breaks, as a way of supporting families. Chapter 4, *Going to Kinship Care* focuses upon children and young people placed with extended family members and friends.

Chapter 5, *Safeguarding and Supporting*, on the second theme, 'safeguarding children', discusses the findings from research exploring the effectiveness of child protection practices and procedures in response to children exposed to domestic violence or drug and alcohol abuse within their families.

The third theme, 'vulnerable adolescents' is explored through the findings presented in Chapter 6, *Caring and Educating*. Its specific focus is adolescent learners who have a range of emotional, behavioural and social difficulties.

Chapter 7, *Advocating and Participating*, on the fourth theme, 'user involvement', discusses the findings from two studies: the participation of disabled children and young people, and advocacy for looked after children and young people, and children in need.

The final chapter revisits the substantive topic, *Quality Matters in Children's Services*. It brings together those findings and ideas that either go across the Overview studies, or have wider implications, for the development of quality Children's Services. In this sense, the chapter represents the main learning from the Overview studies. This includes an exploration of: what the aim of quality Children's Services should be – stability, well-being, resilience?; the quality of care and well-being – exploring the association between the quality of placements and outcomes for children and young people; and the contribution of practice to quality services. The chapter concludes with a discussion of how those working in Children's Services can 'make quality happen'.

Chapter 2

Coming and Going

They don't understand the effect it has, keeping moving you; they should've worked with me. I used to think it must be me, I thought everyone must hate me, move her on. I lost loads of friends. I had loads of social workers too … it makes you feel bad about yourself. You wouldn't do it to a normal kid so why should I be any different?

(Sarah, no permanent base in care)

I will stay here all my life until I get my own house, move in with my girlfriend and have babies.

(Daniel, settled in care)

Introduction

Children and young people come into care for different reasons. Some are abused and neglected by their parents. Others have problems when they are teenagers growing up – such as getting into trouble at home, in their neighbourhood or at school. More globally, other young people may be seeking asylum from war, oppression or extreme economic deprivation. Whatever the reason for their entry to care, their family life has been disrupted. Those who were meant to care for them, who were meant to provide them with a secure attachment, have, for whatever reason, let them down.

In this context the assumption has been that the primary goal of care is to provide these children and young people with permanence or stability in their lives, through a speedy return home, adoption, a longer-term foster care placement, or preparation for adulthood. If this goal is achieved, it can provide the foundation for emotional development including a secure sense of identity and personal fulfilment. Conversely, young people who experience a lot of further disruption whilst in care – as distinct from planned moves which may be positive – are likely to have far more problems whilst in care and poorer outcomes at the time of leaving care.[2] A long shadow may be cast on their education, health and emotional well-being, especially in comparison to their peers who have not been looked after.

Yet, for too many young people in care, stability remains elusive. Studies of young people leaving care during the 1980s, 1990s and 2000, show that about a third experience four plus moves and about ten per cent of these young people have as many as ten or more placements.[3] Currently, about 13 per cent of young people have three or more placements in a single year and only two-thirds of young people who have been in care over two and a half years are likely to remain in the same placement for two years.

At the national level, the introduction of the *Quality Protects* programme, including the performance assessment framework, was recognition of this challenge – no mean task given the variation in local council strategies, policies, funding priorities and practices, as well as the diverse and changing nature of care populations. If councils could improve stability this would: *'ensure that children are securely attached to carers capable of providing safe and effective care for the duration of childhood'* (QP, Objective 1).

Also, at a policy level, the Government's Adoption Reform Programme, following the Prime Minister's Review of Adoption in 2000, and the enactment and ongoing implementation of the Adoption and Children Act 2002, have raised the profile of adoption as a permanence option for looked after children in recent years. This has resulted in increased numbers of looked after children and young people being adopted in England (from 2700 in 1999–2000 to a peak of 3800 in 2004–2005, and 3300 in 2006–2007). Although too early to provide a firm assessment, the impact of the introduction of Special Guardianship Orders on adoption numbers may prove significant over time. Perhaps, more pertinently, the implications of these orders, as a pathway to permanence, will need to be researched.

As detailed in Chapter 1, the introduction of the Public Law Outline, from April 2008, as well as revised statutory Guidance, is intended to enhance permanence for children and young people, by reducing delays in child care proceedings. Finally, in respect of improving stability, policy commitments in the *Care Matters* implementation plan include: piloting ways of enabling young people aged 16–18 to remain in stable placements (Right2Bcared4), and for those aged 18 plus, to remain with their foster carers; training for foster cares in responding to difficult and challenging behaviour; and piloting social work practices, and a social pedagogy approach in children's homes.

In terms of research, it is perhaps surprising, given the status of attachment theory in child care policy, as reflected in the first objective of *Quality Protects*, as well as in social work training and practice, that there has been little empirical work specifically in relation to the attachments of looked after children and young people. Earlier research, applying attachment theory to fostered adolescents, has shown the difficulties many of the young people had in accepting help, or committing themselves to close relationships with their carers, often as a result of rejection by their parents. They were found to be either highly dependent on others, or highly independent, keeping the people who were often important to them at arm's length, especially during their journey to adulthood.[4]

More recently, research into the outcomes of young people leaving foster care has found that a strong attachment to at least one adult is associated with good outcomes (as defined by foster carers, young people and a measure of well-being). This attachment could be with a member of the birth family, foster family, or their partner or partner's family.[5] Recent work has also suggested that different attachment relationships – as distinct from the earlier focus on a single attachment – can contribute to different domains of development, such as encouraging education and leisure interests. And also that the quality of knowledge and information that children and young people are given about their families and backgrounds contributes to their sense of 'connectedness'.[6] In this context, an understanding of attachment, including different patterns, can guide practice interventions.[7]

The Pursuit of Permanence

How far is this goal achieved by the English care system? The first of the core studies, *The Pursuit of Permanence*, attempts to answer this question. It does so by exploring the movement and stability of children and young people within the care system, following in the now distant footsteps of Jane Rowe and her colleagues' 1989 seminal study, *Child Care Now: A Survey of Placement Patterns*.[8] Like *Child Care Now*, it is a very large study, drawing on both quantitative and qualitative data, in relation to 7399 children who had been looked after by 13 local authorities in the course of a year, the last day which fell between 31 May 2003 and 30 June 2004. More specifically, it paints a nationally representative picture of placement movement by taking account of the children and young people – who they are, what they need and want; their care careers – why they enter, how long they stay, and why they leave; the types, purposes and patterns of placements; their outcomes – whether children are settled, happy, behaving and getting on well at school; and the reasons why the care system works as it does. The latter includes the effects of social work teams and differences between local authorities on children, not previously researched.

It is a study of movement which provides a moving picture. This study shows that the care system is, in the main, about 'intended movement', achieved through short-term or medium-term placements, with the aim of returning children home, or placing them for adoption, or the long-term aim of 'care and upbringing', or preparation for adulthood. As outlined in Figure 2.1, *The Pursuit of Permanence* paints a diverse picture, comprising six relatively distinct groups of children and young people: young entrants; adolescent graduates; abused adolescents; adolescent entrants; young people seeking asylum and disabled children.

43%
0–11 years

Young Entrants
Abuse and neglect
60% lead to adoption or placements
focussed on care and up-bringing

43%

57%
11–18 years

26%

Adolescent Graduates
• Abuse and neglect
• Difficulties at school
• Challenging behaviour
40% of 16+'s had placements
which lasted more than 2 years
33% had lasted for less than a year

9%

Abused Adolescents
• Abuse and neglect
• Challenging behaviour
• Difficulties at school
49% had placements which lasted
less than 6 months

14%

Adolescent Entrants
• Relationships at home
• Challenging behaviour
• Difficulties at school
60% had placements which had lasted
less than 6 months

5%

3%

Young People Seeking Asylum
• Behaviour
• School
40% had placements which had lasted
less than 6 months

Disabled Children
• Challenging behaviour
40% had placements which had lasted
less than 6 months

Figure 2.1 Profile of children in care. From The Pursuit of Permanence: A Study of the English Care System. Dissemination material, prepared by Simmonds et al., BAAF.[9]

But what is constant is the belief of the social workers in the 'family ideal', pursuing permanence through 'lasting, homely placements with parents or foster carers close to the child's own home and provided by their own authority'.

The study found that around six out of ten of the 'young entrants', 'adolescent graduates' and 'disabled children' had placements that were meant to lead to adoption or to give care and upbringing, whereas the comparable figures for 'adolescent entrants', 'children seeking asylum' and 'abused adolescents' were much lower. Consistent with these findings, adolescent entrants, abused adolescents and children seeking asylum were far more likely to have placements that had lasted less than six months than the other groups. For young people who remained in care, it was the adolescent graduates who were likely to have longer placements: just under 40 per cent of those young people who were over 16 were in a placement that had lasted for two years or more, whereas in none of the other groups were as many as a quarter of young people in foster placements that had lasted this long. Also, just over a quarter of the adolescent graduates who were over 17 were in placements that had lasted for five years or more.

The study also showed that achieving permanence through adoption was, in the main, restricted to children coming into care under five – only 23 out of more than 4500 children first looked after over the age of five were adopted. Achieving permanence through a return to the family home varied with time since arrival in care. Just under half of children who started to be looked after would leave within a year and two-thirds of those returned home. Among those who had been looked after for a year or more, only around five per cent aged 11–15 were likely to leave, and only about one-fifth of these went home. The research also showed that many of those going back home did not stay there – half of those over 11 had more than one admission to care. Local authorities who returned higher proportions of children home had, on average, higher numbers of children with repeat admissions. Also, children and young people who returned to care were more likely to be doing worse than others of similar age at first admission. The researchers comment:

> These features of the care system resulted in a build up of children who were not going to leave in the near future but who were not, in the end, going to have a long-term stable placement. This is a key challenge. The aim of policy must be to reduce the number of these children, while seeking to ensure that those who are in long-term placements are doing well and those who are not are nevertheless as secure as possible.

How, according to this study, might greater permanence be achieved? A major implication of this study is that the differences between the six groups identified, in relation to age, personal characteristics, developmental needs and pathways, high-light the need for different responses – or what the authors call 'different policies and service frameworks'.

Returning children home – placement with kinship carers and adoption

Consistent with the findings of Jane Rowe's 1989 study, captured by her 'leaving care curve' (also, see Chapter 3), this study also found that successful returns home usually happen within six months and practice should aim at making this work. Early assessment and planning is essential, balancing the complexities of safe-guarding with a return home. If a return home fails and young people come back into care they have very poor chances of being adopted and are highly likely to experience further movement and disruption in care and have poor outcomes. The research showed that children who were least likely to go home were the most vul-nerable in relation to their age, disability and having been abused or neglected. Children who came from families where there was domestic violence or drug and alcohol abuse were as likely to go home as other children but more likely to return to care.

The analysis of the quantitative data suggests that assessment should focus on the reasons for coming into care, especially abuse and neglect, the age at entry to care, any behavioural difficulties and whether rehabilitation had been tried before.

Promoting Quality: Return Home

Adrienne returned home due to positive work completed, co-operation and positive contact which demonstrated the warmth and emotional bond between the parents and all the children. (Reviewer)

Adrienne, aged six, is at home following four months in care. As the social services see it, she was looked after as the result of domestic violence and neglect. Her father abused amphetamines and this fuelled his violence. Adrienne sees things differently. She feels that she was looked after to give her mum a rest. Adrienne thinks it was a good idea that she came into care, and liked both her foster placements.

The plan from the beginning was that Adrienne should return home. This, however, was not to be at any price. At the time of her move to a new foster family return home was considered but not tried since it was felt that the parents had not yet changed enough. Nevertheless Adrienne's move into care seems to have given the parents a shock. The father has given up his amphetamines, the warmth between parents and daughter has shone through and Adrienne has gone home. Adrienne is on the child protection register (something she is said not to want).

Everyone agrees that the current situation is a good outcome. As the reviewer sees it, the plan proved possible because it was agreed on all sides and consistently followed. Neither the reviewer nor the social worker feels that anything else should have been done. They therefore have no recommendations to make.

In addition, domestic violence, drug abuse and challenging behaviour within the family are predictors of failed rehabilitation. Successful placements included those where children did not accept the need to be looked after and had not been abused, and working with a parent on a court order.

The case studies suggested that there was a need to consider a wide range of placements – not just with mothers. Care by fathers, extended family and friends also proved very successful. But authorities who returned more children home than others also had a high proportion of re-entrants to care. Teams were also likely to return children home if they saw the post-care support as good. The qualitative analysis of the case studies suggests that good practice involves realistic assessment, clear planning, a commitment from all the stakeholders, carrying out the agreed plan within the time-scale, carers who support the plan, and maintaining continuity including links with siblings and school.

Adoption can also be successful in providing permanency for young children. However, when it fails it can be devastating. In the study, adoption was virtually only available for children who first entered the system under the age of five. Older children, those with siblings, as well as those who are disabled and from ethnic minority groups were least likely to be adopted. The fact that almost all the adopted children were first looked after under the age of five does not mean that they might not be adopted when older. In the study, a third of those adopted were aged five to nine, and six per cent were ten or over. Nationally, the age range of children being adopted during the year ending 31 March 2007 was: 150 under one year old; 2100 (66.6 per cent) between one and four years; 880 (28 per cent) between five and nine years; 160 (5 per cent) between 10 and 15 years; and 10 (0.3 per cent) aged 16 and over.

Promoting Quality: Managing Adoption

So we invested in adoption, we got some very good managers in who would perform very well elsewhere and we set them high targets and high standards and I think they probably felt that they were well-supported, that they'd got enough people in the team to do a good job. We employed a half-time communication specialist with a dedicated brief around family placement and adoption and she's helped our adoption enquiries increase by a 100 per cent and our fostering enquiries by 25 per cent. So … you know, all of those things came together and … a lot of sweat and hard work really. (Manager)

We're very committed to achieving permanence for children quickly and I see all the papers that go to adoption panel… you can monitor the timescales through that route… good practice is around establishing clear protocols between ourselves, the courts, around the care proceedings process… there's a big commitment around twin tracking… I do think it's an issue about the workloads of staff as well… So we not only went for an additional social worker… but also for an additional admin worker. (Manager – in another authority)

The main implications from both the quantitative and qualitative data included the importance of well-staffed adoption teams, with clear policies and investment in advertising and recruitment of adopters. Procedures should ensure that adoption is considered in all care plans for children where return home is not an option and that these are given due status by 'signing off' at an appropriate level. Also, more twin or 'parallel planning' should be considered by authorities – so that if family rehabilitation fails adoption could be progressed. Carers should also be considered as adopters and in doing so, attention should be paid to their concerns over income and a loss of support.

Providing shared care

In this study, it was estimated that 40 per cent of children who came into care had been looked after before. This included children whose return was planned as a form of 'shared care', those whose return was seen as a 'failure' of rehabilitation, and those whose return was seen as 'likely'. Shared care was successful when regular breaks were planned and took place with the same carer, and combined with other forms of support. But it was least successful when the care was for a prolonged period of time with different carers. The researchers suggest that more use could be made of support foster care for disabled children, many of whom were offered no placement other than a residential one. They cite a very successful example of a disabled young person having a combination of residential care, support care with known foster carers and care at home. When rehabilitation with parents broke down, moving back into care was seen as more devastating than moves within the care system. These returns seem to be experienced as less destructive when the children returned to known carers – in a sense another form of shared care. Preventing high risk returns is important, as detailed in the measures outlined above.

Assisting adolescents

The Pursuit of Permanence identified different groups of adolescents who had different needs and required different forms of assistance.

First, there were young people who had a 'secure base' in care. The case studies showed that some young people were happy where they were placed, felt secure, wanted to remain in their placements and had the amount of contact they wanted with their birth families. Permanence had been successfully pursued and they were likely to be able to 'move on' from care successfully.

A second group included young people seeking asylum and older teenagers who had fallen out with their parents. They both needed what the researchers described as a '*launch pad*' to adulthood. Both groups liked having their own room and assistance from a committed adult to help them with education, employment and practical help, if needed. In addition, young people seeking asylum wanted help in tracing their family and other relatives. Both valued remaining in their placement where they were settled. Suggestions from the qualitative analysis for a successful launch included the importance of inter-agency links, maintaining a base, and having assistance from reliable adults.

The third group were described by the researchers as having no reliable base. Many of the young people within this group had a high degree of movement and disruption whilst in care, experiencing placement break down and moving between foster care and residential care placements. Disturbingly, as the researchers

Promoting Quality: Moving On

Brian clearly adores Barbara and her family and speaks of all of them in the highest terms. The move to independent living holds no fear for him and he sees the change of living location as no bar to his continuing relationship with Barbara and family. (Reviewer)

At five Brian had a brief spell in the care system followed by around five years at home where he became the sole carer for his chronically ill mother. This caring came to involve 'inappropriate intimate' care and Brian was seen as emotionally and physically neglected and abused. He was therefore looked after again for two years around the age of 11. The carers were 'not nice'. Brian became their scapegoat, reported physical abuse and finally ran away to his mother where he remained. Brian remembers this time as a difficult one. He had around 10 short respite placements including one in residential care. In retrospect, he is quite clear that 'it was best when I was at home'. Around two years ago Brian's mother's illness became terminal and she entered a nursing home.

At this point Brian moved to live with Barbara his current carer who regularly took him to see his mother whilst she was in hospital. As Brian sees it, it is really good that Barbara has met her. Barbara is 'just like a mum' to him and this is his home although he will be moving out in the next year or two. When asked if this worries him he says 'not at all', it is only fair that someone else gets to live with Barbara as she is so good and besides, he is only going to be moving down the road so will continue to pop in all the time. Brian says that Barbara has promised to buy him a washing machine for his flat. In the meantime he remains in college where he is doing well on a three-year catering course.

comment: 'estranged from their families and uncontained within the care system some reached a situation where they had, effectively, no place to be'.

The study highlighted the lack of 'treatment' for this group. It was only planned for one per cent within this age group, in comparison to 11 per cent in Jane Rowe's 1989 study. Proposals, arising from the study include 'treatment foster care' which provides clear and consistent boundaries within a warm positive relationship with a foster carer supported by a clinical team, the use of short-term accommodation as crisis intervention and planning, and 'shared care', as discussed above, and the development of adolescent support teams to work with young people when they present problems in their families. Also, some of these young people will need a place to prepare them for adulthood.

Other young people were not committed to their placement. For some of these young people the abuse and neglect they experienced cast a long shadow – they were unable to trust or become close to adults. Others felt abandoned in placements that they loathed or regretted the loss of past placements they had liked. Others were in placements which were officially short term and to which they were reluctant to commit. So what can be done?

The study showed that finding a placement where the young person felt a sense of belonging, and maintaining it, depended on the quality of the carers, the commitment of the child, clear planning, the presence of siblings and the child being happy at school. But it was likely to be disrupted by behavioural problems and a lack of commitment to the placement. The implications of these findings for the carers included the need for better support and training in dealing with young people's challenging behaviour and identifying and nurturing successful long-stay placements. For some children and young people it was important that they were assisted to come to terms with their family situation, removed from damaging placements and helped with their education so that they settled at school.

Wider policy considerations raised by the study included: taking decisions about long-term care as soon as possible; listening to children's views about placements – to avoid placements not working out; giving far more recognition of the parenting role of foster carers, especially in terms of status, decision-making, training and relief breaks; and using 'time out' support or respite care to support good placements that may disrupt from time to time. It is also important to give disabled children and young people more choice of placements, both foster and residential care, not just the latter and perhaps sometimes in combination. Also, the researchers suggest that young people, during their journey to adulthood, may be helped by giving them the opportunity to remain with their long-term foster carers, as well as to receive assistance from them. It may also be helpful for disabled young people, who need ongoing support, to continue to live with their carers, by a seamless 'transfer' to adult services.

Reducing movements and providing more permanence in care

In highlighting the 'intended movement' within the care system, across the different groups of young people identified above, the researchers pose the question 'could there be less movement within the system?' They found that nearly half of the placements in any one year were short term, whilst half of those in their second or third year had placement with medium-term aims, such as preparation for adoption or long-term fostering. Overall, only about 40 per cent of placements were planned as longer term, with the aim of 'care and upbringing', and these were mainly for children and young people who had been looked after for more than three years.

Social workers tended to view placements as successful when they met the 'family ideal', and this was, in the main restricted to adoption, return home or longer-term foster care. By their criteria, difficulties in achieving this ideal included residential care for disabled children, the lack of 'matched' placements for black and minority ethnic children and for young people with challenging behaviour.

COMING AND GOING / 39

Promoting Quality: Planning for Permanence

The foster carers are ace. (Connor)

Connor is now 11 and has been looked after in one placement for six months. His admission was precipitated by his family's eviction from their house, but followed a long period of preventive work in response to his mother's and her partners' chaotic, drug dependent, life-styles fuelled by criminal activity. His mother is currently in prison and her current partner has refused to co-operate with social services. There are no plans for Connor to go home unless his mother changes her life-style, 'which to date she hasn't'.

According to Connor lots of things have happened since he has been looked after by his foster carers ... and 'they are all good'. His placement is 'perfect'. He likes the playstation, the food, his bedroom, getting to choose his own things (choosing his own bed means to him that he is staying). He has started a new school and got into the football team. He has had a birthday and got the new 'England official strip' which according to Connor is 'really dear and is his to keep'. Connor feels lucky to have been in the same placement. He talks about the other foster children and the changes they have had.

Connor is sad about what happened, but glad he is safe. In an ideal world he would like his 'mum to come out of prison, stay off drugs and think of the kids first'. He might then consider living with her but would want to stay in frequent contact with his foster carers. Counselling with a local project is helping him to give up his feelings of responsibility for his family without losing his love for them. He likes seeing 'nanna, mum, mum's boyfriend, my sister and my aunt ... until I am grown up or my mum changes in lots of ways. I just want to stay with my foster carers.' Since admission he has grown six inches in six months and put on 1.5 stone. It is said that he has never looked so happy or content.

The researchers suggest that intended moves may be reduced by broadening the scope of some initial placements, to take children with different needs and for varying lengths of time – thus avoiding the need for interim placements before a final placement is found. Also, there is a need to increase the number of foster placements for disabled children, matched placements for black and minority ethnic children, and placements for young people with challenging behaviour.

The study also shows that local authorities vary in the number of 'care graduates' over the age of 16. Their case analysis revealed different levels in young people's commitment to their care placement, from a sense of belonging and happiness to a rejection and misery, the latter often associated with very unstable care careers. Unsurprisingly, temporary or residential placements did not attract the same commitment as long-stay in foster care. However, the major influence on being settled was the quality of care and the young person's allegiance to their placement. In this context, they recommend that longer-term foster placements should be given the same priority for support as adoption and placements at home, and young people settled in placements should leave care as young people leave home, gradually, with a chance of return and back-up support from those who have been looking after them.

Measuring outcomes

In assessing outcomes for children and young people the researchers used measures of both stability and well-being. As they noted, 'children do not want to stay with carers with whom they are unhappy. They do not want to leave placements where they are doing well.'

The three stability outcomes (derived from official indicators) were: whether the child had three or more placements in the year; the proportion of children who had been looked after continuously for four years or more who had been fostered with the same carer for the past two years; and the proportion of children under the age of 16 who had been looked after continuously for two and a half years or more and who had been in the same placement for the past two years or who were placed for adoption. The 'doing well' measure was calculated from the social worker ratings of 'emotional well-being', 'behaviour', 'positive adult ties', 'being settled in current placement', 'getting on in education or their occupation', and 'being safe and doing well'. What were the main findings?

First, children over 11 who moved a lot showed more challenging behaviour, were less likely to do well at school and were more likely not to want to be in care than others of the same age. However, this was not the case for those who were under 11.

Second, the study showed that there were differences in placement outcomes. Generally, young people had higher well-being in foster care placements. However, when account was taken of the differences between children's backgrounds some of the differences between foster and residential care disappeared. The researchers also warned of being cautious in this assessment – 'we thought it unsafe to assume we had fully taken account of their backgrounds'. Residential placements were seen by social workers a being of higher quality when they were not within the local authority. Also, social workers commonly saw placements with parents on a care order as achieving their purpose. Children and young people were more likely to do well in these placements if they did not want to be looked after and they did not have a need code for abuse.

Children placed with 'family and friends' also had higher well-being scores, and their placements lasted longer and were seen by social workers as more success-ful than other placements. The case studies showed their strengths 'naturalness, continuity, the commitment of family members and the maintenance of family ties'. However, the case studies also showed the down side: the poor health of grandparents, the low income of many of the carers, their lack of experience in coping with challenging behaviour and in dealing with conflicts between carers and birth parents.

Measuring the quality of placements

The researchers also developed two measures of quality: first, a measure of the quality of placements based on ratings by social workers; second, separate ratings by supervising social workers and others of the quality of foster carers and residential units. They found that the quality of placements and the quality of foster carers were both strongly related to their measure of 'doing well', and that the higher the quality, the better the outcome for children and young people. Both these measures were also related to the length of placement where the child was over 11 and the placement was intended to last. The quality of residential units was also related to stability and how well children and young people were doing in terms of their education.

Local departments and social work teams

The study showed that there were great differences between departments in their use of placements, including the proportions returned home, adopted, fostered, living with 'family and friends', and entrants who had previously been admitted to care. There were also variations between departments in the placement stability measures identified above. Through a combination of policies, central procedures, panels and monitoring bodies, cultural changes and resources, departments and teams could bring about changes in the range and choice of provision. However, once a child was in placement, it was the quality of that placement that had a far stronger impact on 'doing well' than either the department or social work team.

- Having an integrated service framework for different groups of children and young people who enter and leave the care system.

- Identifying educational difficulties when they arise in families and in children and young people's placements.

- Having clear arrangements between schools and children's social care for early interventions.

- Having clear arrangements between schools, Child and Adolescant Mental Health Service (CAMHS) and children's social care for assisting young people with emotional and behavioural problems.

Figure 2.2 Integrated working: issues arising from research

Conclusion

The Pursuit of Permanence shows that the care system has different purposes for different children with different needs. It usually begins by providing emergency, remand, or short-term care. It then *pursues permanence* or stability by returning children home, through adoption, by placing them with extended family or friends, providing 'shared care', or providing for their 'care' and 'upbringing' in foster care or children's homes. Care may also become a 'launch pad' to adulthood for later entrants to care. In describing the way the care system works, the study also provides a context for the other studies included in this overview, each of which focuses in depth on a different group and pathway, or a practice across the different groups, as outlined in Figure 2.3.

The Pursuit of Permanence	Sub-group studies included in Overview
Young entrants, entered care under 11 and were:	
Adopted	
Reunified with their birth family	*The Reunification of Looked After Children with their Parents*
Placed with kinship carers	*Kinship Care: Fostering Effective Family and Friends Placements*
	Keeping Them in the Family: Outcomes for Children Placed in Kinship Care through Care Proceedings
Returned or kept at home through planned support care	*Support Foster Care*
	Participation of Disabled Children
Adolescent graduates, entered care under 11 and remained in care	
Adolescents with difficulties	*Educating Difficult Adolescents*
	Child Protection, Domestic Violence and Parental Substance Misuse
Adolescents, entered care aged between 11 and 15	
Adolescent entrants, challenging behaviour	*Educating Difficult Adolescents*
Abused adolescents, more challenging behaviour	*Educating Difficult Adolescents*
Children and young people seeking asylum	
Young people and services across different care groups	
Disabled young people	*Participation of Disabled Children and Young People*
Children at risk through domestic violence, drug and alcohol abuse	*Child Protection, Domestic Violence and Parental Substance Misuse*
Seeking user views	*Advocacy for Looked After Children and Children in Need*

Figure 2.3 Care groups and pathways

In reflecting on the impact of the *Quality Protects* programme, the researchers note that most managers and team leaders 'were overwhelmingly positive towards the initiative within which the indicators are embedded'. It was seen as a very positive way that central Government could support improvements in Children's Services, through clear objectives, underpinned by evidence of good practice, the investment of resources, and accountability for the implementation of agreed plans. However, managers also had had concerns about the performance indicators being used as clear guides of good practice and therefore unambiguous measures of council performance.

The researchers' findings generally reflected this position. The strengths of the indicators lay in highlighting key issues, directing managers' attention to actions that might be taken, especially in response to groups, and raising questions about practice arising from the performance data. In this context, they had a significant contribution to 'assisting an authority to become a "learning organisation" and thus enhancing its contribution to the welfare of looked after children'. The weaknesses of indicators as measures of performance, identified by the research team included: unreliable data; difficulties in interpreting indicators for different groups of children; the influence of indicators on practices which are not good or bad in themselves; possible perverse effects of indicators on individual practice and potential innovation; the lack of correlation between performance indicators and the quality of service provided by the authority.

In furthering *The Pursuit of Permanence*, the researchers distinguish between the decisions that are taken about children (e.g. whether they should remain in care) and their relationship with those who look after them on a day-to-day basis. The evidence suggests that councils find it far easier to influence decisions than they do to influence the children's day-to-day relationships. Social work teams also have a critical role in implementing council policies and hence decisions – it is essential that they own the policies and that they are adequately resourced to carry them out.

Clearly decisions such as those they make on the type of placement and length of time in care are crucial. It is important that there are ways in which they can be systematically influenced. Nevertheless, the researchers conclude 'the quality of placement is by far the most important influence on the child's well-being'. Their recommendations aim to ensure both that more children are in 'the right placement' and that these placements are of high quality.

In order to influence the decisions that are taken the researchers recommend:

• Reducing intended moves by: broadening the scope of some initial placements so they were able to take children of varying kinds and for varying lengths of time thus avoiding the need for interim placements before a final placement is found; increasing the availability of local placements able to take black and minority ethnic children and young people with challenging behaviour; and keeping some young people until they are ready to move on.

- That high priority should 'continue to be given to ensuring return home where appropriate but this requires careful assessment of the relevant risks, good practice and appropriate resources'.

- Early and thorough assessment of the way a placement is working out so that children are not left for a long time in placements where they are unhappy and which fails to meet their needs.

- Placing more children in 'family and friends' care in a structured and planned way. This will require an assessment of needs and capacity, involving different adult and Children's Services (including, education, health, domestic violence and drug abuse services), clear planning and ongoing support.

- The importance of having clear policies on adoption; investment in advertising and the local recruitment of adopters; adequate staffing of 'adoption and fostering teams'; procedures that ensure adoption is considered in all care plans for children where there is no permanence plan for return home and these are 'signed off' at a senior managerial level; 'parallel planning' for children returned home; and being prepared to consider adoptions by carers and to deal with their likely concerns over loss of income and support.

- More use should be made of brief and short-term 'shared care', with particular attention to the need to maintain continuity of carers. Disabled children and young people should also have the choice of more shared foster care arrangements so that disabled teenagers do not spend all their time in an institutional environment.

- That adolescents who had great difficulty in trusting adults and those presenting very challenging behaviour whilst at home or in care may benefit from skilled or 'treatment' interventions. Their carers should be given more assistance in coping with the teenagers' problems. However, a positive change is only likely to succeed if continuity in 'a benign environment' is maintained when young people either return home or move on.

- That younger children who are not adopted or who cannot return home or benefit from other alternatives such as remaining with or moving to carers, residence orders or special guardianship orders, should be provided with permanent placements. These should be given the same support as adoption and placements at home and the young person should be able to live on with their carers after 18 years of age.

- That young people settled in placements should leave care as other young people leave their family home.

In order to increase the quality of placement the researchers recommend:

- A determined programme of research and development into the impact on placement quality and outcomes of the selection, training and support of carers and residential staff.

- The development of systematic programmes of quality assurance that use the day-to-day experience of children, social workers, independent reviewing officers and other key staff to assess the quality of placements.

- The systematic use of this information in making placements and commissioning.

- A shift in priorities of those inspecting foster and residential care so that there is a greater focus on assessing the efficacy of the quality assurance systems for placements.

Questions for Children's Services
Strategic

- Are you able to identify the way children and young people enter and leave the care system, having policies and integrated service frameworks, including education and health, for different groups of children and young people?

- How can your policies ensure that children and young people have their developmental needs met in order to achieve the *Every Child Matters* five outcomes?

- How can interventions to families be better managed in order to reduce the numbers of looked after children over time?

- What measures do you have in place for identifying, recruiting, supporting and evaluating high quality placements?

Operational

- This chapter highlighted that the 'ethos' surrounding the social work team had a significant effect on how they progressed the work with children and young people and the outcomes they achieved. How can you ensure a positive ethos prevails in each team?

- Many troubled teenagers had frequent moves in care, often characterised by fostering breakdowns. How do you recruit and support foster carers, including greater use of evidence-based models such as treatment foster care, in coping with young people who present very challenging behaviours, and what additional services, including education and health, are provided for young people?

- As detailed in this chapter, since the fieldwork for *The Pursuit of Permanence* was carried out during 2003–2004, the Government has overhauled and modernised the legal, policy and practice framework for adoption. The Adoption and Children Act (2002) underpinned the Government's drive to improve the performance of the adoption service and to promote greater use of adoption when it is right for the child. This reform programme has resulted in increased numbers of looked after children and young people, in different age groups, being adopted. However, the research did show wide differences in the likelihood that children with similar characteristics would be adopted in different councils. Have you considered the recommendations (fifth bullet point above) identified by the study, and issues concerning the timeliness of adoptions?

- Could you make more use of returning children home, kinship care and support foster care to provide greater stability?

- Many later entrants to care had the most entrenched difficulties at school, and, conversely, being settled and getting on well at school was associated with placement stability. How do schools in your authority identify educational difficulties when they arise in birth families and care placements, and what arrangements do you have in place between education and children's social care for integrated working?

Practice

- The research highlighted the number of unplanned moves and placements for some young people in care. What would assist you in reducing the number of unplanned moves for children in care that you are working with? How can your department support this?

- The research indicated that kinship placements were able to provide for some children a degree of stability in care. How best can you support these family placements to safeguard children?

- How are you involved in multi-disciplinary working, including, with education and Child and Adolescent Mental Health Services (CAMHS), to assist troubled teenagers?

- How can you be better supported in your role in pursuing all forms of permanence for children in care?

Chapter 3

Going Home

Mum's got better. I prefer it here than anywhere else, I think I'm more understanding.

(Young person, settled back at home)

I went downhill big time, all the anger and hurt inside of me, I was just letting it out.

(Young person, difficulties on returning home)

Introduction

Most social workers try very hard to keep children out of care, or if that is not possible, return them to their family home as soon as they can. The 'family ideal' is the constant in *the pursuit of permanence* – even though the families of children in care have, for whatever reason, been unable to care for their children.

Both research findings and official data show that many children do return home from care within a relatively short time, less than six months or a year, but as time goes by their chance of leaving care drops. This pattern, known as the 'leaving care curve', initially identified by Jane Rowe and her colleagues in their 1989 research study *Child Care Now*, has been validated by *The Pursuit of Permanence* study as discussed in Chapter 2. In *The Pursuit of Permanence* the researchers found that there was a rapid reduction in the numbers remaining in care during the first 50 days. But after a year the chance that a child or young person would leave was very low. Just under two-thirds of children who did return home on leaving did so within six months. By contrast, only a fifth of those who left the system after spending a year in it returned home.

However, as a comprehensive review of the research on reuniting children in care with their families indicates, we need to distinguish between the duration of care at a *descriptive* level and its application as an *explanatory* concept.[10] Despite received wisdom, there is no research evidence that the passage of time *per se* does or does not increase the likelihood of reunification. Other factors such as early planning, parental motivation and strength of attachment, may also play a part during the initial stage of separation. In a similar vein, it has been assumed that parental contact *per se* is likely to contribute to reunification. However, the research review evidence cited above, shows that what matters is the nature and quality of parental contact including the quality of attachment between the parent and child, the joint wishes of the parent and child for reunion, parental motivation, participation in the return process and a willingness by the parents to receive help through planned social work intervention.

In contrast to the volume of research on children who are adopted, or living in foster care or children's homes, there has been relatively little research on children who return home from care, including whether they remain at home or subsequently return to care. Three research studies carried out in England between 1998 and 2006 reported return rates to care of 37 per cent, 40 per cent and 52 per cent. In *The Pursuit of Permanence*, a return to care was more likely when there were family difficulties, behavioural problems or the child had a disability. Other studies have highlighted the parent's mental health problems, social isolation and the lack of support networks, as contributing to re-entry to care.[11]

Recent research has shown that children and young people returning from foster care were significantly more likely to be abused than those who remained in care, and just under a third of the return home sample were re-abused. The same study showed that those children who were returned home had worse emotional and behavioural outcomes than those who remained in foster care or were adopted.[12]

A consultation project with young people who returned to their families in two local authorities highlighted their perceived lack of influence over the decision-making process, except where they forced the issue by voting with their feet – a plight that should be prevented by the strengthening of the role of the Independent Reviewing Officer (IRO) in the Children and Young Persons Act 2008: each child and young person will have a named IRO whose responsibility it will be to find out their views prior to any review. The consultation project also found that young people welcomed ongoing support, especially from former carers with whom they had a positive relationship, as well as more preparation and support for their families where they returned to difficult circumstances. Young people returning home may also feel let down and experience as much movement and instability as young people living independently. For some young people a return home not only fails to provide permanence, it may also fail to protect them, or assist them to achieve educationally – three of *Quality Protects* national objectives.[13]

The reunification of children and young people with their birth families, as well as different ways of supporting families to care for them is the focus of two of the core studies: a Bristol University study, *The Reunification of Looked After Children with their Parents: Patterns, Interventions and Outcomes*, which will be referred to as the *Reuni-*

fication research; and research carried out by the Thomas Coram Research Unit *Support Foster Care: Developing a Short-Break Service for Children in Need*. This will be referred to as the *Support Foster Care* study.

The Reunification research

What factors contribute to a successful return home or lead to further movement and disruption? It was this gap in our knowledge that the *Reunification* research aimed to address. It explored the patterns and outcomes of returns home by a two-year follow-up study of 180 looked after children, aged from birth to 14, who were returned to their parents between January and December 2001, excluding those returned within six weeks. A third of the children were looked after under the age of five, over a quarter were aged between five and ten, and just over 40 per cent were aged between 10 and 14. The sample was drawn from six local authorities and the data collection methods included case file reviews and a qualitative study based on interviews with 34 parents, 22 social workers and 19 children. The study aimed to describe the children's experiences, before, during and after their return home, and to identify what made a return home successful or unsuccessful.

The *Reunification* study found that the children who were to go home had come from very problematic backgrounds. As many as 90 per cent of these children and young people had experienced abuse or neglect in families, in which domestic violence, substance abuse, or both, were prevalent. Just over half of their mothers had spent time in care when they were younger or had been victims of abuse or neglect themselves. Just under two-thirds of the children had experienced between five and ten 'parental or child adversities' prior to coming into care: the former included domestic violence, drug misuse, prostitution, multiple partners, poor parenting skills and parental death; and the latter, maltreatment or exposure to a Schedule 1 offender. Only five children (3 per cent) had not experienced any of these adversities.

Over half of the children had been on the child protection register and two-fifths had been previously looked after. They were mainly looked after because they were at risk of further abuse or neglect, or because of their parents circumstances and problems. Before returning home, just under three-quarters of the children were placed in foster care, eight per cent were living with relatives or friends, and 13 per cent were in some form of residential setting. The average duration of these placements was just over ten months, ranging from under one month to more than five years.

For just under two-thirds of these children contact with their families began within two weeks of them becoming looked after. For others it commenced once the parent was discharged from hospital or treatment, when the child had been placed closer to home, or after inflamed family situations had calmed down. Most of these children (82 per cent) saw their parents weekly or more and support was provided for contact in two-thirds of cases. The quality of contact was variable, ranging from 'positive' to 'poor', and a small number of children were abused. Prior to their return home most of the children increased their contact with their parents, including overnight stays for almost three-quarters of the sample. A return home was only planned for about 40 per cent of the sample, and time-limited assessment recorded for another 45 per cent. Just under half of the sample (48 per cent) returned home following a court decision or pressure from the parent, the young person or their care placement.

The researchers found that legal status at entry to care, age, previous child protection history and previous care history all significantly influenced the initial plans made for the children. Just over a third (35 per cent) of the children were returned home without any assessment of their situation, or after only an initial assessment (8 per cent), despite their highly difficult backgrounds before coming into care. The researchers comment:

> The oldest children, who had typically oscillated in and out of care, frequently absconded or were returned home before a care plan had been formulated. It is concerning that this particularly problematic group of children received the least oversight whilst looked after.

The 'agency neglect' of these young people's needs is also identified in the analysis of serious case reviews 2002–2005, in the 2008, DCSF Research Report, *Analysing Child Deaths and Serious Injury Through Abuse and Neglect: What Can We Learn?*[14] The analysis showed that a quarter of the 161 children who died or who were seriously injured, were over 11 years, including nine per cent who were over 16 years of age. Although most of these 'hard to help' young people had a long history of involvement from children's social care and other specialist agencies, including periods of care, by the time of the serious incident, 'little or no help was being offered because agencies appeared to have run out of helping strategies' (p.83). In highlighting a number of 'agency response' problems, including failures in assessment, sustaining involvement, identifying agency involvement, and a lack of co-ordination of services for young people in transition, the report recommends: 'more creative, more responsive services for these young people … specialist adolescent support teams in the community, with good links with a range of agencies appear to offer the best opportunities for engaging these hard to reach young people' (p.83).

The *Reunification* researchers found that children's initial care plans influenced whether assessment took place. Over half of children had a fuller assessment, either multi-agency (43 per cent), social services (34 per cent), or another agency alone (23 per cent). Almost three-quarters of the multi-agency assessments were considered to have been sufficiently analytical and useful to safely inform a return decision, compared with only a third of the assessments conducted by social services alone or two-fifths of another agency alone. The researchers comment, 'this is not a finding about the competence of these assessments but highlights the complexity of the family issues and the need for a multi-disciplinary approach to assessment'.

Having high quality multi-agency assessments (including adult and Children's Services) was critical to both successful returns home and the range of support services provided. For example, the research team found that where multi-agency assessments were conducted, children were more likely to be returned home safely and that better assessment led to better service provision. Also, where no work was carried out with any family member, as had happened in just under a quarter of cases, problems tended to persist when children returned home. The researchers also found that the conditions for a successful return home were more likely to be set after the family situation had been assessed, and assessment was also linked to future support being provided to families.

Promoting Quality: Assessment, Condition Setting and Multi-Agency Working

Teenagers Jane and Ted had a volatile relationship and there were concerns about drug use. When Jane was 16 she became pregnant with Ryan – who was placed on the Child Protection Register as an unborn child after Ted assaulted Jane. The couple separated soon after Ryan was born but two months later Jane contacted Children's Services, having again been physically assaulted by Ted whilst she was holding the baby. The situation remained inflamed and an emergency police protection order was made on Ryan who was taken into care. The next day a core assessment was begun. Ted was taken into custody for the assault, but upon his release threatened to abduct Ryan.

At a child protection conference the following month it was decided that a residential assessment of Jane's parenting skills and ability to protect Ryan should be undertaken. Jane was committed to the residential assessment and demonstrated an increased ability to protect Ryan and meet his needs. She was also adamant that she wanted no further contact with Ted or any other violent partner and this was made a requirement for her to return to the community with Ryan. On completion of the assessment the residential staff, health visitor and probation officer all agreed that Jane and Ryan should return home. The return was subsequently successful.

The researchers found that in a quarter of cases no services had been provided for the parents during the time their child had been looked after. And where returns were planned preparations for returns were only made in a third of cases. In the researchers' assessment, in only a quarter of cases had all the problems been addressed before the children went home, in just under quarter (22 per cent) none had been addressed, and in just over a half (52 per cent), some of their problems had been dealt with.

Promoting Quality: Through Multi-Agency Work

Chris had been in care because of his difficult and aggressive behaviour at home. His first return home had not worked out because little had changed, but after another nine months in care his second return at the age of 12 was successful, partly as a result of the range of supports for reunification and partly because he had learned to control his temper. Chris had been involved in anger management sessions whilst in care and had found ways to control his aggression and a psychiatrist prescribed Ritalin which was effective. Regular respite care was provided to support the return for the first year which Chris enjoyed. His social worker also took Chris out for chats and was 'brilliant' and gave his mother back-up. His mother said of the social worker, 'He was there for me. I could phone if I had any problems... I wasn't on my own. They would help... They were like family in the end.'

Chris was also able to talk to his mother's new partner. In addition, the school was very supportive to his mother and a school counsellor saw Chris. He was enthusiastic about his Year Head who was his mentor and confidante and gave him a great deal of support. Chris explained, 'I've learned self-control... Care made me mature more quickly... I love being at home now... I'd hate to go back into foster care.'

Social workers or other professionals expressed concerns about a third of the returns. Also, in the qualitative study, parents talked about doubts over their ability to cope, and some children said they would have preferred to remain in care. Just under two-thirds of the children returned to the same carer although a quarter returned to households where one adult had joined or left, and a tenth joined new households. There was a high recurrence of drug (42 per cent) and alcohol misuse (51 per cent) in families to whom the children returned, and these behaviours were also associated with higher rates of social isolation, financial problems, poor parenting skills, marked instability, anti-social behaviour and poor home conditions – the range of risk factors identified in the families of older young people in the analysis of serious case reviews discussed above. But only five per cent of parents were provided with treatment to help them address their substance abuse.

The *Reunification* research also relates to the *Quality Protects* Objective 2, to ensure that children are protected from emotional, physical and sexual abuse, and neglect. The researchers found that just under half of the children (46 per cent) who returned home were abused or neglected within their families – exactly half the number who had been maltreated prior to being looked after – although nearly two-thirds (62 per cent) remained with the abuser. Children of substance abusing parents were more likely to suffer incidents of abuse or neglect than children of parents without misuse issues. The researchers found that poor parenting skills were the greatest predictor of child maltreatment during the return period, followed by drug and alcohol abuse.

By the end of the two-year follow-up period, just under half of the returns home had broken down and the young people returned to care. Over half of these young people were returned home again and half of these new returns broke down. Altogether, two-thirds of the children experienced one or more failed returns, including a third who had oscillated in and out of care twice or more. Children found oscillating between home and care a very negative experience. Moreover, a quarter of the continuing returns to the family home were rated of poor quality for the child.

Promoting Quality: Through Multi-Agency Support

Irena's mother, Mrs Black, had mental health problems and received three months of treatment in psychiatric hospital before her daughter Irena, then aged three, was returned to her. This return succeeded because of the support provided by the mental health team, children's social worker and Mrs Black's parents as well as by the school. After Mrs Black was discharged, the psychiatric hospital provided good after care and Mrs Black had the telephone number of the hospital so that she could go in whenever she wanted to talk to a staff member and she also had support from her parents and friends. Her social worker visited weekly which the mother found helpful, 'I could talk to her about how I felt.'

Mrs Black was by then receiving a Disability Living Allowance so that her income increased. Also, a befriender was arranged for her. She commented, 'The quality of help and support you get is very high in Greentown. The social worker is there if I need anything and the help is excellent.' Nonetheless, Mrs Black commented, 'It took a long time for Irena to trust me again… I think she needed me to prove that I loved her.'

Irena was fortunate to have been able to continue at the nursery school she had attended before entering care which provided continuity for her. Irena saw the social worker weekly for the first six months after reunification and her school worked closely with the other agencies in providing support and help to Irena and her mother.

In concluding their study, the researchers identify the factors that emerged as significantly related to return stability and success.

Children who returned home on a supervision or care order (or who were on the child protection register) were significantly more likely to experience return stability as compared to those who were voluntarily accommodated. As the researchers explain, 'those on court orders received more and overall better support from Children's Services and other agencies, were more often set conditions which they needed to fulfil before children returned and were subject to close monitoring'. Those who were least likely to be assisted were young people who were accommodated, older and mainly adolescent. Consistent with these findings, black and minority ethnic children (BME) had a greater likelihood of return stability, as this was associated with the higher proportion who returned on court orders (57 per cent), and thus who were also more closely monitored and received more and better support, compared with non-black and minority ethnic children (37 per cent).

There was an increased risk of return disruption for children and young people who entered care without their brothers or sisters, and for those with a previous failed reunification. Evidence of poor parenting skills prior to return, previous physical abuse and parental ambivalence about return, were also associated with an increased likelihood of disruption. Return stability was associated with a move to the 'other parent', who generally was found to have fewer problems than the parent from whom the child entered care, or when there was a positive change, such as a new partner becoming part of the family.

During return a third of the children were not close to either parent and a considerable number said in interview that they found things difficult at home, felt sad, confused or angry, yet a third had confided in no-one after return. They found oscillating between home and care a very negative experience. When asked what help they needed, parents prioritised: treatment for substance misuse combined with clarity about the consequences of their taking no action about their addiction; help with behaviour management; earlier recognition of their difficulties with their children; respite care and direct help for children (such as mental health assistance and mentoring).

Also, support from schools was important. The local education authority provided educational assistance to over half of the school age children – just over 40 per cent were underachieving at school, whilst a quarter had a Statement of Special Educational Needs. School changes, lack of friends and getting behind with their schoolwork, could result from moves between home and care. The researcher interviews with parents and children showed that this support could be considerable, could also include support for parents and was seen as contributing to the success of returns. During return home, poor attendance and exclusion was significantly related to disruption.

As detailed above, monitoring of parents' situation before a return, good quality multi-agency assessment, preparation and supervision, setting of conditions after return, are all associated with return stability. Generally, parental pressure for a return home was associated with success. However, when young people pressed for reunification – or discharged themselves home – there were more disruptions. There was also evidence that where foster carers, or other caregivers, had developed supportive relationships with parents there were significantly fewer disruptions.

Perhaps, not surprisingly, given the findings detailed above, a comprehensive set of services, addressing problems prior to reunification, providing specialist support for the parent or child, and any additional services that were needed, is associated with significantly more stable returns. This included high quality direct work – 'reunification' social work: 'arranging comprehensive packages of services, liaising with other agencies, attending meetings, and conducting direct work – social workers sometimes visited daily … when children were returned'. Again, as described above, some of the major problems faced by social workers included the high recurrence rates for parental alcohol and drug misuse when children returned home; working with 'unco-operative' parents, and the difficulties associated with 'borderline' cases, where it was finely balanced as to whether the child would be better off at home or in care.

Finally, the researchers carried out a regression analysis to determine which individual factors were most predictive of return stability (returns not disrupting) and success (the quality of the returns). In terms of stability, the key factors predicting returns not disrupting were: having addressed all the problems that had led to care; multi-agency supervision of the return; the child being close to at least one parent figure; receiving good parenting during the return and the parent not being socially isolated. Being of black or minority ethnic origin also predicted return stability, principally because most of the BME children were on care orders and, as noted earlier, children on care orders had fewer disruptions than others.

A re-analysis by age showed that the key factors predicting return stability for the older children (aged 11 or older at return) were: adequate preparation for return, informal support for the parent or young person, the young person not having serious attachment problems and return to a changed in household or home. Subsequent analysis showed that one of the most influential factors in return stability and success for all children, but particularly for adolescents, was the local authority the child lived in, reflecting wide variations in practice.

Lack of return success was related to adolescent returns where young people had shown behavioural difficulties, including substance misuse, before entry to care and to younger children who were hyperactive or had emotional problems. The predictors for return success (that is return quality) from the regression analysis were very similar to those for stability. They were the child returning home under care proceedings; moving to a new address or changed household; highly competent social work before and during the return; that the original problems did not arise again; the child was close to a least one parent figure; received good parenting during the return and was not beyond parental control. A re-analysis by age had broadly similar findings to the analyses for placement stability, except that return success for the younger children (aged 11 or younger at return) was additionally predicted by the child having been assessed prior to return and lack of domestic violence and conflict with parents during reunification.

Support foster care

> I've had parents who've come back to me and said without the service they would have cracked up and put the children into accommodation, or gone under. (Support Carer)

Helping children to remain with their families at times of difficulty or stress, and thus avoid the need for longer- or medium-term care, can also reduce unnecessary movement and disruption. One way of doing this is by the provision of 'support foster care' schemes, to give short breaks for children with another carer, combined with help for parents. The characteristics of this kind of support are described in *Care Matters: Time to Deliver for Children in Care*: 'parents retain responsibility … children are not removed from home … the service can be infinitely flexible, and offer help in the short term or over longer periods when needed. Support carers can also act as befrienders and mentors, helping young people with specific difficulties' (p.28).

To date the research into this form of support has been mainly descriptive, highlighting the use of accommodation as a form of family support and the focus on working in partnership with parents. There has also been little research on the views and experiences of carers. Qualitative research in this area has found that short-break carers are motivated by the desire to help children and parents under stress, often as a direct result of their own positive experiences. In the disability field, it has also been shown that short-break carers have concerns about training, support, and levels of payment.

Section 20 of the Children Act 1989, and the accompanying Guidance, provides the legal framework, stipulating that no placement can be for more than four weeks, the total duration in a year must not exceed 90 days, and all placements must be with the same carer. In England, the majority of these placements, just over 70 per cent, are used to support the families of disabled children. A far smaller number (28 per cent) are used to help other families who need relief, and official data indicated that since 1999 this form of provision had been in decline. It was in this context that the Thomas Coram Research Unit was commissioned to carry out their study of *Support Foster Care*.[15]

The main aims of the research were to provide information on the extent and nature of support foster care schemes in England, including their objectives and ways of working with children and families. More specifically, the study aimed to find out more about the barriers, legal or otherwise to establishing such schemes, as well as how local authorities were overcoming these barriers.

The main methods used to carry out the research included a short screening questionnaire, sent to all 150 local authorities in England, initially generating a 31 per cent response rate but leading to additional methods to identify authorities with support schemes. Fourteen authorities were identified from the screening survey: six with support schemes; two in the process of setting up such a scheme; and six authorities who did not have a support scheme. They were generally representative of different local authorities. Semi-structured telephone interviews were carried out with key staff in these authorities and three schemes were studied in more depth through visits and focus groups with support carers. Finally, co-ordinators of six community childminding schemes providing care for children in need were surveyed, to explore the impact of new Ofsted arrangements, allowing childminders to provide overnight and home care, and the potential for community childminding schemes to develop into support care. The fieldwork was carried out between March and August 2003.

What were the key messages? To begin with, the research showed that there was a lot of variation in the size and scope of the schemes, in terms of the number of carers and the number of children cared for by them over time. However, whatever the variation, a defining feature was their flexibility in responding to the needs of the child and the family. Regular weekend breaks, daytime care (for pre-school-aged children and those excluded from school), regular overnight stays during the week, as well as full-time care for short periods for parents who had longer-term needs were all on offer.

Promoting Quality: A Flexible Support Package

A particular strength of support care identified in the study was that flexible arrangements could be made to suit the particular circumstances of children and families. Although short breaks were usually provided to prevent children needing to become looked after, they could also be used alongside periods of accommodation to ensure greater continuity and stability for children. For example, in one authority support carers were also approved to provide short-term foster care. This was particularly useful in the case of two young children whose mother had severe but episodic mental health problems. They were provided with short breaks on a regular basis by a support carer who also looked after them full time when their mother was admitted to hospital. The local authority was committed to continuing this arrangement for as long as it was needed, and the scheme manager described how much the placement meant to the children:

> 'They hadn't been able to talk to their social worker about it, about their fears and loyalty to their mother, but because they know this carer very well, and know that they will go back and see her again when their mother is ill, they are actually able to talk to her quite a lot about it. At the review, the little boy said "I can talk about my mummy and she hugs me," and it was lovely, knowing that those children got that support.'

An important part of the support care approach was working in partnership with parents. In addition to meeting the needs of the family and availability of carers, the researchers observed that 'most support care schemes had a strong philosophy of time-limited acute service delivery, to discourage parental dependence on the service'. The support was usually offered for no more than nine months, and very much aimed at helping families to overcome temporary difficulties and problems. As such, it was often offered as part of a package of support, including help from social workers or other practitioners.

Promoting Quality: Assisting Reunification

In another case, a support carer was able to help a young woman to build a better relationship with her stepmother, both whilst the girl was living at home and when she eventually returned to the care system. This improved relationship meant that the young woman was better supported by her family, even though she was no longer living at home. Support care could also be used as part of a plan to return children home to parents under a supervision order, and enable them to rejoin their families earlier than might otherwise have been the case. One scheme co-ordinator commented that 'in the past – before the scheme – I think social workers might have been very cautious and the child would have remained looked after by full time carers.'

The main barrier to developing support care schemes was seen by local authority managers as 'the priority placed on recruiting carers for the mainstream fostering service, and a fear that support care schemes might create competition for an increasingly scarce resource'. However, the study found that this was not the case. In fact, support carers were drawn from a pool of people who were not able to be full-time foster carers, or who would have left the fostering service rather than continue full time. In some cases, opportunities for part-time care actually provided a pathway to full time fostering.

A second perceived barrier was the low priority afforded to these schemes, reflected in the level of funding, including any additional support and training that would be needed by carers who were supporting families as well as caring for children. Although support carers were very committed to their work there was dissatisfaction with poor pay, as well as a feeling that their service was not valued as much as it should be by social services.

In terms of the legal framework, the researchers reported that most scheme co-ordinators were unhappy that support care was provided under Section 20 of the Children Act 1989, and thus required children to be legally 'looked after'. Their concerns included the potential to 'alienate parents – the stigma associated with 'looked after' status – and the extensive paperwork required when a child becomes accommodated'.

The co-ordinators wanted to be able to offer an accessible service and some raised the issue of whether it would be more appropriate to provide support care under Section 17 of the Act, as a form of 'family support' rather than as 'accommodation' under Section 20. The researchers found that most schemes had adopted some variation of the *Looking After Children* procedures as a regulatory framework but there was wide variation in practice in respect of medicals, reviews and care plans. However, the researchers also found that some community childminding networks had started to offer a similar short-break service, including overnight care, but with no requirement for childminders to be registered as foster carers.

Promoting Quality: Arranging Short-Break Support

A number of support care projects had well-developed placement procedures which fitted well with the philosophy of partnership with parents. Once a family was referred to the service, *Looking After Children* forms in some cases modified would be completed and a carer sought who could meet the family's needs. Co-ordinators placed great stress upon the importance of the parent and child agreeing to the placement. The placement procedure usually began with the identification of a suitable carer, followed by an informal visit by parents to the carer's home 'to get a feel of what the place is like'. Sometimes parents brought a friend with them for support.

A family placement visit was then arranged where the children were introduced to the potential carer. The carer or family could refuse a placement after the initial visit, and an attempt would then be made to find another carer for the child. Although a placement agreement was drawn up specifying the duration of service and dates on which care would be offered, in practice almost all co-ordinators and carers noted that some degree of flexibility could occur. The carer and parent might agree to swap a weekend session for a mid-week visit (with the co-ordinator's approval), or social workers might ask carers to vary the agreed arrangements in order to facilitate some other piece of task-focused work with the family, or to give a stressed parent a period of respite earlier than had been planned.

- Including in your Children and Young Person's Plan the contribution of children's and adult services to reunification work.

- Carrying out multi-agency assessments, involving both children and adult services.

- Recognising the contribution of schools to the success of reunification in assisting children and supporting parents.

- Identifying and arranging 'comprehensive packages of support' and 'liaising with other agencies', as a key component of reunification work.

Figure 3.1 Integrated working: issues arising from research

How effective were the schemes in preventing children being accommodated? As only one of the schemes kept detailed records, and none of the others had information systems providing monitoring or outcome data, it is not possible to answer this question drawing on quantitative data. However, in respect of the scheme which collected systematic data, out of 250 referrals over a year only seven (just under 3 per cent) went on to be accommodated. In addition, many of the co-ordinators gave examples of families, supported by the service, coping with severe problems in the community without breaking down. This was collaborated in focus groups by the views of the support carers. There was also evidence that parents generally valued the service highly and that they felt involved in and consulted about the support they and their children received.

In relation to *Quality Protects*, the researchers highlighted the contribution of support foster care to promoting continuity and stability for children. This included examples of children having the same support carer on a regular basis, children and young people being helped to build and repair family relationships, and the use of support care as providing a bridge to reunification from care. *The Pursuit of Permanence* study (Chapter 2) also found that regular breaks with the same carer where the child new the 'base' was successful, whereas 'shared care over a prolonged period with different carers … appeared to lead to insecurity'. In several authorities, support carers were also registered for short-term mainstream fostering, so that in an emergency a child who had accessed support care could also be accommodated with a carer they knew. There were also examples of short-term carers being approved as longer-term foster carers for children for whom they had provided short breaks.

Conclusion

Promoting stability through returning children to their families, and by the provision of support foster care, so they can remain at home, is the focus of the two studies discussed in this chapter. As detailed above, there is clear evidence that both are able to meet Objective 1 of the *Quality Protects* programme. But to maximise their potential and ensure the best outcomes for children and young people will require improvements in policy and practice.

- The *Reunification* study showed that many of the serious concerns that led to children coming into care had not been addressed before they returned home. They were returning to the same problems with a high risk of re-admission to care, and the attendant costs.

- There is a need for more multi-agency assessments, including adult and Children's Services, to identify what needs to change before children return home.

- This should lead to a plan with clear targets, commitment of all the key players to its implementation, monitoring of standards, and the service interventions required both prior to, and during the return.

- Schools are a major source of formal support to parents and educational assistance to children and young people, and their intervention can contribute to the success of reunification.

- High quality 'reunification' social work contributes to stable returns. This included: 'arranging comprehensive packages of services, liaising with other agencies, attending meetings, and conducting direct work – social workers sometimes visited daily … when children were returned'.

- The *Permanence* researchers echoed these findings, also adding the need for contingency planning as part of the assessment process, having high quality carers 'who were able to sympathise with the parents, support the child and work with the social workers'. They also stressed the need for continuity, the importance of children keeping links with siblings, avoiding a change of school, and ongoing contact with their families.

- The *Reunification* research also showed that there are likely to be benefits if foster carers and residential workers could be more involved in preparing children and in providing follow-up support to them and to their parents after reunification. This is an area of practice that might usefully be further developed.

- The *Reunification* research showed that the most vulnerable group were adolescents who were accommodated on a voluntary basis. They were the group who were least likely to have detailed planning arrangements and receive appropriate services. Their treatment contrasted sharply with children subject to the jurisdiction and scrutiny of the courts who had higher levels of assessment, supervision and services.

- Parental substance misuse was a serious problem and related to higher levels of maltreatment, poor parenting and domestic violence when children were returned home. Social workers require more training in working with substance misusing parents, and parents need more access to treatment facilities.

The main implications from *Support Foster Care* study for the development of an effective service were:

- The need for support foster care to have a far higher profile within the range of local authority Children's Services, including its incorporation into mainstream budgets.

- For carers to be offered a better package of support and training – 'the provision of similar support to that enjoyed by mainstream carers, such as carers' group meetings, access to equipment, 24 hour "on call" support and regular supervision should be no more costly than when provided for full-time carers, and would help to ensure that support carers feel valued and enabled in their work'. The researchers also suggest that support carers should be offered more in-house and focused support carer training involving the key stakeholders.

- More information about the purpose of schemes, as well as clearer lines of communication, would reduce unrealistic expectations from social workers. This has included expecting support care to provide emergency placements, or care for children with severe behavioural or psychological difficulties, for which they were not trained, equipped or supported to undertake.

- In order to demonstrate the impact of their service, authorities will need to collect systematic monitoring and outcome data on the children and families provided with support care.

Questions for Children's Services
Strategic

- How does your Children and Young People's Plan demonstrate the priority you are giving to reunification work, including the contribution of children's social care, education and other service providers?

- What resource is allocated to actively support the rehabilitative work with families when children and young people become looked after?

- Does the Director of Children's Services monitor the reunification support plan and assessment for all looked after children and young people who return home, and how does this inform your reunification policy?

- What mechanisms are in place to test and review whether local threshold levels for entry to care are too high, too low or just right?

Operational

- How are you ensuring that children and their birth families receive a multi-agency assessment, including providers of children's and adult services, before they return home?

- Have you considered whether a Family Group Conference model could be used for reunification planning and support?

- What multi-agency training, including adult and Children's Services, do you have in place to improve integrated working and practice in relation to reunification work?

- Do you provide clear information on the role and purpose of your support foster care service, and how have you integrated your support foster care service within your mainstream fostering or family support service?

Practice

- How are you addressing the serious concerns that led to children and young people being looked after, before they return home?

- How are you assessing and meeting the needs of families where there are substance misusing parents?

- How much post-reunification support is offered to children and their families once they return home?

- Have you assessed what additional services may be needed for adolescents with behavioural and emotional difficulties, and for their carers in managing their behaviour, and the implications for integrated working?

Chapter 4

Going to Kinship Care

I get on really brilliant with them … she's lovely, she really is. She treats me like one of her own daughters.

(Young woman living with a friend's parents)

With your auntie you know who you are living with and you can trust them and they are related. It's not a stranger you are going to, you know them since you were little and you can trust them with whatever you do.

(Young person living with auntie)

Introduction

Kinship care has a warm feeling about it. Even on first sight, it would seem to have the potential to offer children and young people emotional stability, by remaining within their extended family, or by living locally with family friends. After all, the care of the orphaned and illegitimate child by relatives, within their manorial community, has a long history, dating back to the feudal period. More recently, the Guidance to the Children Act 1989 stresses, if young people cannot remain at home, placement with relatives or friends should be explored before other forms of placement are considered. In response to the proposals contained within the 2007 White Paper, *Care Matters: Time for Change*, the Children and Young Persons Act 2008 will enable local authorities to provide improved financial support for family and friends carers, as well as reducing obstacles for kin carers in applying for Residence and Special Guardianship Orders. More globally, Article 16 of the UN Convention of the Rights of the Child, recognises the importance of the 'family environment … for the full and harmonious development' of the child's personality.

Recent research, mainly descriptive, is also generally positive about the benefits of kin placements, in providing attachment and continuity of care, through placement stability, contact with birth parents, keeping siblings together and maintaining school and community links, thus respecting social, cultural and ethnic diversity. Kinship care may also be seen as a positive choice both by children and parents. In these different ways kinship care may contribute to emotional well-being, providing children and young people with a secure sense of identity, and a coherent story about their lives, without them having to think about it too much.[16]

Also, in the UK, recent research has shown that there are few differences between the children and young people placed in foster care and kinship care – they are likely to have similar needs and difficulties. Problematic areas arising out of research studies have, in the main, focused on the failure of local authorities to assess and plan placements properly, and provide adequate financial, practical and ongoing support, especially in comparison with foster care, rather than raise questions about the benefits of kinship care. Concerns have also been raised about the variations in the categorisation employed by local authorities, as detailed below.[17]

There is also evidence that kinship care arranged *informally* by family members and friends when provided with extra support can be effective in promoting stability for children and young people 'in need', and reducing the need for them to be looked after by the local authority.[18]

It is surprising then, given this potential, that only about 7000 looked after children in England, 11 per cent of the total, were placed with 'family and friends' in England in 2007 – although we don't know how many children are living in kinship care arranged *informally* by family members and friends. The numbers of looked after children placed in kinship care have increased since the implementation of the Children Act 1989 provided a stronger legal framework, but only gradually – just three per cent between 1992 and 2003. In some European countries up to three-quarters of children are placed in kinship care.

However, although there have been descriptive studies, as reported above, there have been few recent outcome studies of kinship care that have looked at stability and 'well-being' during childhood, adolescence and into adulthood, especially in the United Kingdom. The Bristol and Oxford studies aimed to address some of the gaps in our knowledge of this area.

Kinship Care: Fostering Effective Family and Friends Placements

The Bristol research, *Kinship Care: Fostering Effective Family and Friends Placements*, aimed to provide information about the characteristics, progress and outcomes of children placed with family and friends; to compare these with a similar group placed with unrelated foster carers; and to explore the factors that contributed to success in these placements. It also aimed to describe the needs of the children and carers. It was carried out through a case file review of 270 children (142 (53 per cent) living with kin and 128 (47 per cent) with foster carers), on a set date (July 2000) and followed-up for two years. The research design also included interviews with 32 kin carers, and with children, social workers and parents.

At the outset the study showed wide variation in the legal categories used by local authorities. This included: looked after children placed with kin in 'emergency' foster placements (Regulation 11, now Regulation 38), converted within six weeks to foster care placements (Regulation 3); private fostering placements with friends, if they lasted longer than 28 days; fostering under Residence Orders (Regulation 3 (5); whilst 'a few received financial support only under children in need arrangements' (Section 17 (11)).

The sample included between a quarter and third of children who had been in placements for up to two years, half for two to six years and the remainder for over six years. Just under half of the children were under ten and most (70 per cent) were on care orders or interim care orders. Grandparents (45 per cent) were the largest group of family and friends carers, followed by aunts and uncles (32 per cent), and a small number of other relatives such as cousins or siblings. The 'friends' group included neighbours, ex-residential workers, former step-parents, teachers and others, representing 18 per cent, or almost one in five of all placements.

In general, *Kinship Care* showed that broadly similar children, in terms of characteristics and needs, were placed with 'family and friends' and foster care placements. However, children with multiple health problems and those who had a parent who had been in care during childhood were more often placed with unrelated foster carers than with family or friends. In addition, significantly more black and minority ethnic children (60 per cent) were placed with unrelated carers than with kin (40 per cent). *The Pursuit of Permanence* study suggested that there were some differences: children placed with relatives were less likely to be aged 11 or over, or to have entered the care system for the first time when aged 11 and over. However, there were only very slight differences in the needs of the children placed – those placed with relatives were more likely to have a 'need code' of abuse and neglect, and less likely to have need codes of disability, acute family stress, or abandonment. Also, two-thirds of the children placed with relatives were for 'care and upbringing' in contrast to 40 per cent of those placed in foster care. The *Kinship Care* study also showed that long-term care was much more often the plan for children placed with kin than for those in foster care.

As regards the characteristics of the carers, *Kinship Care* found that family and friend carers were more likely than foster carers, to be lone carers, live in overcrowded conditions, experience financial hardship and have a disability or chronic illness.

Kin carers were more likely than unrelated foster carers to be struggling to cope with the children in their care (45 per cent kin vs. 30 per cent unrelated carers) and, as a result, in a considerable number of the placements which were continuing at follow-up kin carers were under strain.

Children who were placed with relatives had higher levels of contact with aunts, uncles and cousins and, when they were living with paternal relatives, also with their fathers. However, difficult relationships between kin carers and the children's parents or other family members emerged for over half (54 per cent) of the family and friends carers but for far fewer (16 per cent) unrelated foster carers. In such situations of conflict, family and friends carers often wanted the protection of care orders and the involvement of social services in order to maintain adequate boundaries around contact between the children, their parents and/or other members of the family.

In terms of overall levels of support, significantly more kin carers had little social work support (69 per cent) as compared with unrelated foster carers (47 per cent). The kin carers had a wide range of unmet needs, the most pressing of which was for counselling and specialist help for children with severe and persistent behavioural and emotional difficulties. They also required adequate financial payments, as some were in situations of severe financial hardship, and assistance with contact issues when there were high levels of conflict with parents or other relatives.

In terms of 'well-being', using the ratings from the *Looking After Children Assessment and Action Records*, *Children Placed with Family and Friends* found that after two years, children showed similar levels of general health and school attendance, and more than three-quarters of children in both placements showed improved behaviour. Children with emotional or behavioural problems were likely to receive similar assistance. But, worryingly, they reported that over a third of children in foster care and almost half of those in kin care, those with the most serious problems, were not receiving any intervention. Where information was available on closeness to carers, friendships, social behaviour, and changes in school attendance, this showed that children's progress in both types of placement was very similar.

Promoting Quality: Social Work Intervention

One social worker provided a particularly high quality service to an aunt and the two nephews and one niece she looked after. The social worker visited fortnightly and talked to the children and their aunt separately. When she was off sick this placement broke down and the children were accommodated. As soon as the social worker returned to work she managed to get the placement reinstated. She also arranged for an independent agency respite carer to take the children for some weekends and applied for additional financial help when it was needed. The social worker realised that the aunt's perseverance was a great help to these children and had protected them from having unstable care careers. Her proactive work in turn helped to sustain this family and friends placement.

In evaluating the outcomes of placements, two kinds of outcome were adopted: first, a rating of placement quality which assesses how well placements met the needs of children; and second, placement disruption. Overall, the study found that there were no differences in the quality or disruption levels of kinship and unrelated placements.

Researcher ratings, by the research team, of placement quality showed similar levels: two-thirds of those with foster carers and just under three-quarters of those with family and friends were rated as positive, in which children were seen as happy and developing well. In both settings, placements were of poorer quality when the children's parents had misused drugs. Also, the problems and behaviour of children *before* placement and *during* placement was linked to both disruption and placement quality: children who had behavioural difficulties at home or school, including truancy, poor progress at school, or getting into trouble (e.g. stealing or damaging property) were at increased risk of disruption.

However, there was an important difference in the duration of placements. Kin placement lasted on average ten months longer: three-quarters of children were still in these placements two years from the date the sample was drawn, compared to only 55 per cent with foster carers. But consistent with the findings from *The Pursuit of Permanence*, the higher rate of endings from foster care were intended or planned moves to other placements. Disruption rates (18 per cent and 17 per cent) for both types of placement were similar. However, there were higher levels of placement disruption in kin care when young people were over the age of ten at placement. In contrast, in non-related care, disruption levels were highest for children place between the ages of five and ten.

The approval of family and friends as foster carers was linked to higher levels of stability – most likely explained by the rigours of the approval process, as well as better levels of support and financial assistance. The research also found that placements with family and friends were more likely to last and cope with children's past and present behavioural difficulties – 'kin carers were more likely to persevere beyond the point at which foster carers conceded defeat, even when they were under considerable strain'. However, kin and unrelated foster carers were treated differently when there were serious concerns about the placement: although kin placements were visited more often by social workers when there were concerns, they were far less likely to be offered ongoing support services than foster carers.

Among kin carers, children placed with grandparents were the least likely to experience disruption (8 per cent), as compared with 27 per cent of children with aunts and uncles and 30 per cent with other relatives or friends. This compares with 23 per cent of disruptions for children with non-relative carers. Also, twice as many children returned to a parent from foster care, compared to kin care, reflecting the differences between interim and longer-term placement plans.

Promoting Quality: Help from 'Friends' Care

Ricky had grown up in a chaotic home, physically abused by both his parents and affected by his mother's mental health difficulties and periodic overdoses. At the age of 12 the parents of a friend were asked to care for him for a few days and he remained with them thereafter:

'When we had Ricky he was a pretty sick child really – he slept in the cupboard; wouldn't sleep in a bed – he was sick all the time, anorexic – wanted to kill himself. It was terrible. But I was the right one for him. I would stay up at night with him and we would talk. And it was very, very hard, because the first three years the parents were fighting a lot between themselves, and then the father remarried and I think Ricky found it all very hard to deal with. But you know, I worked through it gradually. Because I would stay up and talk to Ricky, or I would go in when he was crying, and I used to say to him, "Look Ricky, the only one that's getting hurt here is you. You've got your whole life ahead of you".'

Ricky had been in the placement for two years when an assessment was done and he was described as a 'happy, cheerful boy who laughs a lot. His attendance at school is 100 per cent now and he wants to go on to college after school. He is also much more confident in his general demeanour.'

There were only a small number of very poor placements, fewer than ten per cent, in both types of care. But very unsatisfactory placements with family and friends care were found to last significantly longer than those in foster care. The researchers suggest that this was a result of little monitoring by social workers and referrals from the family were often disregarded. They also comment:

> In other situations, social workers had allowed standards to fall considerably below those that would have been accepted for other children, either feeling that they could not readily intervene in ongoing kin placements or thinking that, for children, being with family trumped other difficulties.

Keeping Them in the Family

The Oxford study, *Keeping Them in the Family*, focused on a more specific group of children than the *Kinship Care* study, those removed from their parents' care by the courts because of child protection concern.[19] Also, in contrast to this study, its main aim was not a comparison between children placed with kinship carers and unrelated foster carers. However, there were some over-laps. The *Kinship Care* study did include children who went through care proceedings, and *Keeping Them in the Family* did include a small sample of children who were placed with carers who were not members of their extended family or social network.

Keeping Them in the Family explored the outcomes for 113 kinship placements, following care proceedings, which ended between 1995 and 2001. Four outcome measures were used, derived from Objective 1 of the *Quality Protects* programme – secure attachment to safe and effective carers. These were: placement stability; placement quality; relationship with carers; and child well-being. The study also examined decision-making, contact issues, support for placements and the views of children and kinship carers.

The study was carried out by a case file review of 113 children, 37 interviews with kinship carers, including the completion of well-being measures for adults and children, 24 interviews with social workers in active or recently closed cases, 14 interviews with children and young people, and two interviews with parents. The comparison group was made up of 31 children aged under five years old who had also been the subject of care proceedings brought by the same local authorities during 1995–1998, but who were either fostered or adopted.

How did the children do in relation to the four main outcomes? The researchers reported that just under three-quarters (72 per cent) of placements were either continuing and stable, had lasted as long as needed, or were continuing even though there were difficulties. In relation to just over a quarter that had ended prematurely, half of these children continued to be cared for by either a parent or other relative. Just over three-quarters of these children also had positive and close relationships with their carers, even where the placements had ended earlier than planned.

The researchers also found that most placements were safe, only ten per cent raising child protection issues, mainly concerned with neglect. However, most placements did raise some quality issues, just over a third being free of any such concerns and 20 per cent raising major concerns. In respect of well-being, most children were doing well or reasonably well; only 19 per cent had difficulties in three or more dimensions. Set in the context of these children's adversities prior to placement – which were similar to the comparison group – the researchers suggest that kinship care is viable option which should be promoted, but should be based on careful assessment, including identifying the support needs of carers.

The researchers also explored what contributed to 'poorer' or 'better' outcomes. In respect of the child, better outcomes were found where the child was young, had fewer difficulties pre-placement, had lived with the carer on a full-time basis before and had not asked to live elsewhere. In relation to the placement, better outcomes were associated with a single carer rather than a couple, a grandparent carer, where there were no other children in the household other than the child's siblings and the placement being instigated by the carer. Better outcomes were also found where there had been a pre-placement assessment and a positive assessment of parenting capacity.

However, the researchers found that only the age of the child at the end of the proceedings had an explanatory value across all four outcome areas. But this was

Promoting Quality in Kinship Care

Jason's mum had a longstanding problem with heroin use. Jason spent extended periods of time living either with his maternal grandmother or his maternal uncle, who at one point had a residence order for him. When Jason was 11 years old, his mother became unable to cope with him and he was accommodated with unrelated foster carers at Mum's request when she was admitted to a psychiatric ward following a suicide attempt. Care proceedings were initiated.

Prior to proceedings the local authority had not been aware of any potential carers in the family. The children's guardian, however, initiated a more thorough search, traced the maternal uncle and after a positive assessment Jason went to live with him. When interviewed the maternal uncle commended the great efforts the guardian had put in to finding him and ensuring that Jason remained within his family. Whilst living with foster carers Jason was reported to be a bit 'wild'; he didn't really have much respect for his foster carers and was destructive of his own property. The placement with his maternal uncle and his partner was positive for Jason. His uncle feels that if he hadn't come to live with him and had stayed in foster care there was real potential for him to go off the rails. Jason's leaving care worker concurred stating that he couldn't imagine Jason would have done as well elsewhere. At the point our research was carried out Jason was 17 and still with his uncle and aunt who said he could stay with them until he felt ready to move out.

This case illustrates one of our key findings that previous full-time care by the kinship carer is associated with better outcomes. A positive outcome was achieved for Jason because the children's guardian extended the search for potential carers beyond any that were immediately accessible. It clearly demonstrates the importance of carrying out comprehensive searches to identify potential relative carers, especially if the relative has had previous full-time care of the child, and to 'mapping', at the earliest possible opportunity, the family and social networks of children on the brink of care.

seen as understandable in the context of the child's longer exposure to adversities, and consistent with placements of very young children doing well in other types of placement. However, the study also found that some older children did well in kinship care, where there had been earlier intense contact and a strong ongoing relationship. Most of the young people who scored badly on all outcome measures were very difficult and damaged, and where their carers struggled to handle their problems.

Keeping Them in the Family also looked at some of the key decisions about kinship care. They found that in just over a half of cases where children were placed with other carers, kinship care had not been explored by social workers, although their data showed that there was not an unlimited supply of relatives able to care for

Promoting Quality: 'Having Someone to Turn to'

Paul was placed with his maternal uncle and aunt under a care order. Two years after proceedings ended, because of difficulties with other members of the extended family, Paul and his carers relocated 150 miles away. Children's Services seemed uninvolved in this crisis as the case was unallocated at this point and the family was not linked up with the Social Services department in their new area. From the information found on the files the researcher rated this placement as receiving little support. When interviewed, the social worker gave the same view citing the distance being a bit of a difficulty. Thus in some respects this case exemplifies the vulnerability of out of area kinship placements and the need to establish local support systems. Surprisingly, however, when the carers were interviewed they gave Children's Services ten out of ten for the help they had received and said:

'Just letting us know that they're there to talk to and reassuring us we're not on our own. The (current social worker) is easy to get hold of and I can discuss things with her.'

This demonstrates that kinship carers are not asking the earth in terms of practical support, just having someone to turn to is valued and highlights the importance of carers having a named person available at the end of the phone who they can contact as and when necessary.

children. Carers were often motivated by their existing bonds with the child and sense of familial duty, but were rarely involved by the local authority in formal decision-making processes, and few had a full assessment before a child was placed with them.

Researcher interviews with 37 carers revealed that most of the children they looked after had emotional, behavioural or learning difficulties, and although some of these problems diminished over time, caring was often a mixed challenge – rewards, tensions and restraints. Most of the carers would have welcomed more financial, practical and professional support in enabling them to sustain their care. The findings from the interviews with a very small sample of children (12) revealed a strong sense of attachment and belonging in their kinship care placements. Most had maintained contact with their mother and siblings, and lost contact with their fathers. However, parental contact was likely to lessen over time and problematic contact was also common.

- Including in your Children and Young Person's Plan the contribution of children's and adult services to promoting kinship care.

- Having arrangements with education and health services to identify kinship carers and ensure high quality support services are provided.

- Identifying educational difficulties when they arise in kinship care.

- Having clear arrangements between schools, CAMHS and children's social care for assisting young people with emotional and behavioural problems in kinship care.

Figure 4.1 Integrated working: issues arising from research

Conclusion

Both the studies discussed in this chapter, and *The Pursuit of Permanence* researchers suggest that kinship care is a viable option that should be promoted, given that most family and friends placements can be of good quality, do as well as foster care and promote stability. However, as the *Keeping Them in the Family* researchers point out 'kinship care can deliver Quality Protects Objective 1 for many children but it does not work for all'. In *The Pursuit of Permanence*, the researchers also comment:

> Councils that make comparatively little use of kin placements can look into safely increasing the proportion of kin placements provided they pay attention to the special requirements of these placements for support – this increase is likely to further the emphasis in 'ordinary' foster care on more specialist functions – preparation for adoption, and the maintenance of challenging adolescents.

The main policy and practice issues and recommendations arising from these studies include:

- Wide variation in the range and quality of services.

- The provision of specialist kin or family placement workers and better training for social workers may lead to more kinship care placements, as only four per cent of placements were initiated by field social workers.

- The use of kinship placements may be increased by systematic exploration of 'the kinship option for all children prior to proceedings', through the 'mapping' of significant relatives to explore kinship care at an early stage, and by recording the efforts made.

- The use of family group conferences should be developed as a process for exploring kinship networks.

- The assessment process is critical to selecting and maintaining high quality placements.

- The assessment process should pay attention to the thresholds for approving family and friends carers informed by an understanding of the distinctive features of kinship care.

- The assessment process should identify the support needs of the over fives, their level of difficulties, and the contribution of different agencies, including children's social care, education, CAMHS and other service providers.

- A two-stage assessment process should be considered, in order to strike a balance 'between making a pre-placement assessment and early placement with kin'. This would be an 'early and rapid viability assessment', followed by a 'subsequent exploration with the carers of the wider issues of caring'.

- Disruption review meetings should be held where placements have been terminated, to find out the reasons for breakdowns.

- Kinship carers would benefit from better financial and practical support. Financial assistance based on the assessed needs of the children they care for, and written information about the legal and financial options available to them when they start caring for children, would greatly assist them.

- Kinship carers would welcome more assistance with children's behavioural difficulties, including when problems first arise at school. Truanting was associated with less satisfactory kin and foster care placements.

- Kinship carers would welcome contact planning for birth families, in terms of assessment and ongoing support, especially where there are difficulties for children and disputes with birth parents; opportunities for respite care; the provision of better social work support, including back-up support when a case is closed, and for 'out of authority' placements.

- A national policy framework and Guidance should be considered, which should include the implications for workforce training and the development of best policy and practice.

Questions for Children's Services
Strategic

- Is the promotion of kinship care, as a preventive measure, identified as a priority within your Children and Young People's Plan?

- Has your authority put in place a local policy and practice framework to promote and support kinship care arrangements in order to meet the requirements of the Adoption and Children Act 2002 and the developing *Care Matters* agenda on kinship care?

- Is your policy available on your website and how can kinship carers find out more about local policy and practice?

- What arrangements has your authority made to collaborate with parents and parents' organisations in order to develop policy, for example through local parent forums or networks?

Operational

- What arrangements do you have in place to ensure that kinship care is both actively explored and adequately supported, as an early option to prevent children and young people entering the care system or as an alternative to remaining in foster or residential care?

- How often do you use Family Group Conferences to explore all viable options including kinship care in individual cases?

- What arrangements do you have in place to track and report the percentage of children and young people for whom kinship care is actively explored or put in place as an option?

- What arrangements do you have in place to assess the quality of the ongoing support provided to kinship carers.

Practice

- How have you been trained and equipped to assess and meet the ongoing support needs of kinship carers?

- Does your assessment include the identification of emotional and behavioural difficulties, and where indicated, carry out integrated working with CAMHS?

- How have you been prepared and trained to resolve conflicts, and thus potentially prevent some disruptions, where there are problems between kinship carers and parents or other family members?

Chapter 5

Safeguarding and Promoting

I was not in touch with reality. I used drugs to block out feelings of depression ... because I was using drugs I didn't see the effect it was having on Danielle.

(Mother)

Danielle was left in the bedroom alone and unsupervised with drug-using men in the house ... she was at risk of anything.

(Social Worker)

She (Danielle) had no friends, and there was a lack of extended family support, as they had given up on Mum. They were isolated from society ... there was no routine, no regular meal times and no food in the cupboards.

(Health Visitor)

Introduction

The high proportion of children referred to social services, who were exposed to domestic violence, drug and alcohol abuse within their families, was a major finding to emerge from an earlier overview, *Child Protection: Messages from Research*, published in 1995. Since that time, research studies have shown the prominence of these issues at different stages of the child protection process, including at the time of the initial assessment, at child protection conferences and during supervision. These studies have also shown that children who grow up in families where there is domestic violence, or parental drug or alcohol misuse are at increased risk of significant harm to both their physical health and their emotional development. This may include direct harm to the unborn child, children sustaining injuries in trying to intervene in violent disputes between parents, or children and young people being neglected emotionally and physically through poor parenting. In addition to the implications for their physical safety, there is evidence that such negative experiences may result in damaged attachment patterns and emotional insecurity.[20]

Recent research has shown that domestic violence and parental substance abuse may also prevent families getting the help they need both informally and through the child protection process.[21] As regards the former, there is evidence that such parenting may alienate potential 'family and friends' support networks, who, as the studies discussed in Chapter 4 have shown, may provide stability and good quality care. The child protection process may be influenced by parental reluctance to admit they have a problem and seek help, especially where the perpetrator may threaten the mother or child. In addition, there is evidence that practitioners are less likely to visit violent parents, investigate such cases thoroughly, and have the training and expertise to work with them. Parental hostility to helping agencies was identified in the analysis of serious case reviews as having a paralysing effect on practitioners which 'hampered their ability to reflect, make judgements act clearly, and to follow through with referrals, assessments or plans'[22] (p.90).

Effective integrated working, which involves both adult and Children's Services, has been central to government policy in this field, and is critical to safeguarding children in circumstances where there is range of problems. However, it is an ongoing challenge: different legal frameworks; splits between adult and Children's Services; and different professional cultures, practices and identities, may all result in barriers to inter-agency collaboration. Recognition of these problems and ways of addressing them are explored in *Reaching Out: Think Family* (2007). This includes examples of innovative local programmes, demonstrating that working with the whole family, can assist with problems when they arise, even in families faced with multiple problems. It also stresses the importance of extending *'thinking family'* to the development of an integrated, multi-agency approach across both adults' and Children's Services.

In this context, building on the statutory framework laid down by Sections 27 and 47 of the Children Act 1989, for agencies to co-operate when there are concerns about children's safety and welfare, the Children Act 2004 strengthens the 1989 Act, by placing a duty on statutory agencies to co-operate to improve children's well-being. Also, in response to the *Victoria Climbié Inquiry Report*, organisations and people are required under Section 11 of the Children Act 2004 to make arrangements for ensuring that their functions and services provided on their behalf are discharged with regard to the need to safeguard and promote the welfare of children.

An inter-agency approach is also a foundation stone of the *Framework for the Assessment of Children in Need and their Families* and the introduction of the *Integrated Children's System*. The third joint chief inspectors' report on arrangements to safeguard children, *Safeguarding Children* (2008) found that joint working arrangements, particularly between Crime and Disorder Reduction Partnerships, Children's Services, the police and health services, had been strengthened, although highlighting that a fifth of Local Safeguarding Children Boards had failed to demonstrate the impact on outcomes for children and young people. Finally, at the time of writing, the Multi-Agency Risk Assessment Conferences (MARAC) implementation programme is being rolled out nationally in all of the Specialist Domestic

Violence Court areas, underpinned by Guidance and training funded by the Home Office.

Child protection, domestic violence and parental substance misuse

How effective are child protection practices and procedures in response to children exposed to domestic violence or drug and alcohol abuse within their families? It was this question that the *Child Protection* study set out to address. More specifically, it aimed to: explore how children's social care responded to families where problems required the interventions of both adult and Children's Services; identify the factors that enabled different agencies to successfully work together at the various stages of assessment, planning, service delivery and review; and explore children's and parents' experiences of professional interventions, and identify what they viewed as most helpful.

In pursuit of these aims, six local authorities were selected on two criteria: the type of authority – two London Boroughs, two Metropolitan Boroughs and two Shire Counties were selected; and the extent to which they had developed working practices between children's social care and services working with domestic violence and substance misuse – two authorities that had well-developed working practices, two in the middle range and two with less developed working practices were selected. There were four main sources of information: first a scrutiny of agency plans, Area Child Protection Committee (the predecessors of Local Safeguarding Children Boards) procedures, policy documents and training plans; second, data from 78 practitioners, on their awareness of the above documents, gathered by a postal questionnaire; third, a study of 357 case files, half with evidence of domestic violence and half with evidence of parental substance misuse – in a fifth of cases domestic violence and substance misuse coexisted; and fourth, interviews with 17 parents and relevant practitioners. Cases were included in the sample when a child had been referred for services to safeguard or promote his or her welfare during 2002, and concerns about domestic violence and/or substance misuse were identified at the point of referral or during the initial assessment.

What were the main findings? The analysis of the 375 case files showed that three-quarters of the sample came to the attention of children's social care as a result of referrals predominantly from the police and health workers. The remaining quarter were referred by family members, neighbours and friends seeking help, mostly in relation to children aged over five years of age. Two practice concerns arose at this stage, both contrary to official Guidance. First, in just under half of the cases, practitioners failed to raise concerns with parents before making a referral. Second, in some cases no core assessment had been started on the initiation of s47 enquiries, or by the time an initial child protection conference had been held, although the researchers found that Guidance was more likely to be adhered to once the Assessment Framework was embedded into practice.

The case file analysis also highlighted the vulnerability of the children and young people living with domestic violence and parental substance abuse. As many as three-quarters of the children had unmet needs in at least one area of their development, most (85 per cent) were living with parents who were unable to undertake all key parenting tasks, and also for most children (87 per cent), the wider family and environment were having a negative impact. The research team assessed a fifth of cases as 'multi-problem – that is children were experiencing severe difficulties in relation to all three domains: developmental needs *and* parenting capacity *and* family and environmental factors'. The researchers also identified the *co-morbidity* of issues confronting families. Many experienced a combination of domestic violence, parental alcohol misuse, drug misuse, mental illness and learning disability. Not surprisingly, when domestic violence, parental drug or alcohol abuse came together, the effect on children's lives was more serious.

What was the response of Children's Services to these needs? The researchers found that in three-quarters of cases the initial assessment led to some form of action being taken. But in just under two-thirds of the remaining cases, where no action had been taken, the children were shown to have severe needs in relation to either the child's development, parenting capacity, or family and environmental factors – a failure of early intervention, as the researchers comment:

> This raises the spectre of children identified by children's social care as 'in need' being left unsupported and unmonitored in families who are unable to adequately safeguard or promote their welfare.

How did the agencies work together? The study showed that services for domestic violence and substance abuse were not routinely involved at any stage in the child protection process – the initial assessment, initial child protection conference or planning stage – even when there was evidence of these issues within the family. There was evidence of more involvement in providing services, but this was still in only a fifth of domestic violence cases, and in just over a quarter of cases where there was evidence of parental substance misuse.

The researchers found that the extent to which agencies collaborated depended on the managers' and practitioners' knowledge of different agencies, their willingness to work together, and the perceived quality of working relationships. However, the research showed that the awareness of managers in the six participating local authorities, representing the police, children's social care, education, health, domestic violence, substance misuse, housing, voluntary support and probation, varied both between and within local authorities. The health service was seen as an important organisation to involve when there were concerns about children living with domestic violence or parental substance misuse. The research showed that nearly two-thirds (63 per cent) of the 56 managers outside of the health service said that they would involve one or more parts of the health service, including health visitors, Primary Care Trusts, General Practitioners, midwives and school nurses.

However, the researchers found that most managers failed to routinely involve the education services when children lived with domestic violence or parental substance abuse, despite the crucial role played by schools in referring, monitoring and promoting the welfare of children and in providing information to assess their developmental needs.

Promoting Quality: Strategic Plans and Services

Local authority strategic plans can encourage innovative practice to support children living with domestic violence and/or parental substance misuse. For example, a domestic violence forum plan in one authority, in addition to implementing a large-scale, multi-agency strategy, also included the appointment of a children's development worker, the introduction of an awareness-raising project in several local high schools, plus the publication of articles on domestic violence in the local youth newspaper. A further example of innovative practice was found in another local authority where the domestic violence forum plan established a programme for perpetrators of domestic violence with a concurrent support group for children.

The managers from the different agencies viewed the factors identified below as supporting inter-agency collaboration: understanding and respecting the roles and responsibilities of other services; good communication, regular contact and meetings; common priorities and trust; joint training; knowing what services are available and who to contact; clear guidelines and procedures for working together; low staff turnover. Barriers included the converse of the above, as well as no clear systems to resolve issues of confidentiality, insufficient resources including time, workloads, costs and staffing, a lack of trust, and negative preconceptions of parents with problem alcohol or drug use.

The researchers were only able to interview 17 parents – not the 42 they had hoped for. However, their views were, in the main, consistent with the picture that had been drawn from the analysis of the 357 case files. Most parents had a range of difficulties, including poor mental and physical health, and poor social and economic circumstances. Half of the group had sought help because of concerns about their child's welfare, although the remainder were either unaware that they had been referred, or had not given their consent. Parental satisfaction about the services they received was associated with parents acknowledging their problems, their involvement in the assessment and planning process and being informed about what was happening to them. They valued both practical help and emotional support. In response to being asked what would improve services for families like their own they suggested: paying greater attention to ensuring families understood what was happening and consulting them throughout the process of assessment, planning and intervention; adopting a more honest, open and respectful approach; providing longer-term service provision; and co-ordinating better with other service providers.

Promoting Quality: Working with the Parents

Involving the parents in the process of assessment, listening to what they say and showing respect for them as individuals was found to be essential to developing an honest and open working relationship.

'I could tell the social worker the truth. I had no problem with being truthful, I knew it would be best to be honest.' (Mother, in a case involving domestic violence)

Good relationships between parents and social workers were shown to be associated with parental willingness to collaborate and work with social workers during the assessment process, satisfaction with the outcome of the assessment, willingness to engage with services, and perceptions of whether their situation had changed for the better.

The research team also scrutinised the content of key documents from the six local authorities, including the plans, procedures and protocols, provided by the Area Child Protection Committee (ACPC), Domestic Violence Forum, the Drug Action Team, Community Safety team, and the Children and Families Services. Key points to emerge from their examination included the wide variation between study authorities, and the greater coverage given to domestic violence than parental substance misuse. The researchers also found that ACPC joint protocols did not routinely cover what to do when children live with domestic violence or parental substance misuse. In some authorities joint protocols for information sharing had been developed between particular agencies but there was no evidence of an agreed protocol to which all agencies had signed up to.

As the researchers comment, 'providing plans, procedures and joint protocols will not in themselves bring about the required changes in practice. Practitioners will need training on the underlying principles and how to implement the procedures and protocols.' The review of training plans showed that the higher profile given to domestic violence in the documentation was also found in relation to training. This was reflected in managers' attendance at recent training events, as well as in their understanding of the issues.

The research highlighted the difficulty of direct work with children and families. Alcohol or drug problems may affect parents' understanding of what is happening, what is being said to them, or their ability to recall key information. This requires practitioners having the time to explain and clarify information, often needing several visits, to carry out the assessment process. In addition, parental problems with drugs, alcohol or violence may also make the ongoing practitioner relationship more difficult to sustain.

- Including in your Children and Young Person's Plan the contribution of children's and adult services in meeting the needs of children, young people and families affected by domestic violence and substance abuse.

- Having clear arrangements for collaboration between children's and adult services in carrying out assessments, planning and intervening in families.

- Training and equipping staff in multi-disciplinary work, including information sharing, assessment and intervening.

Figure 5.1 Integrated working: issues arising from research

Conclusion

This study has examined how Objective 2 of the *Quality Protects* programme, '*to ensure children are protected from emotional, physical and sexual abuse and neglect* that, is translated into practice in respect of children who are exposed to domestic violence or drug and alcohol abuse within their families. As the research summarised at the beginning of this chapter shows, these children are often at risk of suffering significant harm to their physical health and emotional well-being. In the *Reunification* study, discussed in Chapter 3, half of the children returned home were abused or neglected and maltreatment rates were highest with substance-misusing parents. It is also evident from this research study and the current policy and practice context that interventions will only succeed if they involve integrated working at each stage of the process, including joint assessments, planning, intervention and review.

The research findings raise a number of key issues for policy and practice aimed at improving the safeguarding of children and young people.

- There is a need for clearer guidelines between the police and children's social care on the referral process. The researchers found that police were likely to notify children's social care of all incidents, and not discriminate between a notification or 'contact' and a 'referral' – 'this practice tends to overwhelm children's social care'. The researchers suggest 'the introduction of the *Common Assessment Framework* could provide a tool to support the police to make more considered judgements and ensure children's social care receive better information about the cases notified to them'.

- More consultation and collaboration with practitioners from adult services, including health, substance misuse, domestic violence and housing, in carrying out assessments, decision-making and planning, is required to respond better to the multiplicity of needs facing families.

- More recognition should be given to the role played by schools in referring, assessing and monitoring children and young people.

- In order to overcome some of the barriers arising from confidentiality and data protection policy and practices, local authorities should build on existing inter-agency protocols for information sharing and ensure that agencies working with adults are invited. The aim of such protocols should be to guide practitioners in making professional judgements about what to share, in what circumstances, and for what purposes.

- In response to the finding that staff were not always aware of services to support children and families experiencing domestic violence or substance misuse, it is suggested that managers need to ensure that the information held on the local authority's service directory, as specified in *Every Child Matters*, is comprehensive, up-to-date and easily accessible.

- The research showed that official Guidance on the procedures to be followed during the different stages of the child protection process was not always followed. This included a reluctance to carry out core assessments on complex cases; core assessments not being preceded by initial assessments; and core assessments not being carried out when enquiries were conducted under Section 47.

- Central management need to support line managers to ensure compliance with Guidance. Children's Services should establish a system for internal auditing of social work case files, carried out by managers not responsible for the cases, and appoint independent chairs for conferences.

- The difficulties of carrying out direct work, including the impact of drug, alcohol and violence, on the assessment process and sustaining relationships, should be acknowledged.

- The study showed that involving parents at all stages is strongly associated with parental satisfaction. This will include practitioners having the time to explain things at the outset, as well as the provision of well-written, informative and accessible brochures and leaflets.

- Parents often felt that insufficient attention was paid to their needs – 'managers need to ensure that assessments identify not only children's development needs, but also parents' acute and chronic difficulties'.

- Children should be given a higher priority in all strategic local authority plans whose primary focus are adults, and that the Local Safeguarding Children Boards, and local authorities Children and Young People's Plans should address the needs of children and families affected by domestic violence and substance abuse.

- Greater priority needs to be given to both training on domestic violence and substance abuse – the latter also identified in the *Reunification* study, including inter-agency training.

Questions for Children's Services
Strategic

- What priority is given in your Children and Young People's Plan to meet the needs of children, young people and families affected by domestic violence and substance abuse?

- How do you know that you have an integrated service in operation across all the elements of children's and adult services, including children's social care, education and schools, CAMHS, third sector organisations working with children and families, police, probation, health, housing and other specialist providers?

- How do you know that your service is effective in identifying and acting appropriately in response to family situations in which children and young people are exposed to domestic violence and substance misuse?

- Does both your Common Assessment Framework and Assessment Framework policies include guidelines for the categorisation of a referral in relation to domestic violence from the police?

- Do your policies mean that adult services are contacted in relation to referrals to children's social care involving substance misuse, domestic violence and housing?

Operational

- What do you do to enable your staff to recognise the needs of children and young people who are living with domestic violence and parental substance misuse?

- What processes do you have in place to support your staff in integrated working and information sharing?

- What do you do to ensure that your staff participate fully in the processes set out in the Assessment Framework processes and *Working Together*?

- What procedures do you have in place to ensure that parents are involved at each stage of the process?

Practice

- What do you do to ensure that children and young people have access to multi-agency support to meet their assessed needs?

- What do you do to safeguard and promote the welfare of children and young people who witness domestic violence and parental substance misuse?

- Are you clear about your agency's protocols in relation to information sharing with other departments and agencies, and trained and skilled in multi-disciplinary working?

Chapter 6

Caring and Educating

Jack had originally entered care as a toddler, had experienced a failed adoption alongside five other placements, before being placed in a local authority children's home. He had been on the family-finding list for nearly four years and was found a foster family. The move was described as having been very positive for him. His early behaviour problems had settled down and his self-harming was improving. Although he was described as 'not academic', and his emotional problems still held him back in school, he was thought to be maturing and his school attainment was improving. This was seen as a result of 'a stable placement', the carers contribution and the one-to-one attention he received: 'He is laying a lot of ghosts – working through difficult experiences with his carers.'

(Researcher interview with social worker)

Children need to be treated more as individuals and not simply looked at in terms of attainment levels. Personal, social and emotional capabilities are closely related to educational attainment, success in the labour market, and to children's well-being.

(*The Children's Plan, Building Brighter Futures*, 2007)

Introduction

Improving the educational outcomes of looked after children, and young people leaving care, has been a central platform of the Government's modernisation programme for Children's Services since 1997. Research findings, as well as official data at the time, had shown that children and young people in and leaving care had significantly lower levels of attainment in comparison to young people in the general population. A study carried out in the mid-1990s estimated that at any one time, just under a third of looked after children were not attending mainstream education, either through truancy, or having been excluded from school. Research studies at that time suggested that successful educational outcomes were associated with placement stability, being looked after longer in foster care, being female and having a supportive and encouraging environment for study – and without such stability and encouragement post-16 education, employment and training outcomes were also likely to be very poor compared to other young people.[23]

In this context, as detailed in Chapter 1, ensuring *that children in need* (Objective 3) *and children looked after* (Objective 4) *gain maximum life chance benefits from educational opportunities*, were key objectives under the *Quality Protects* programme. In addition, Objective 5, '*To ensure that young people leaving care, as they enter adulthood are not isolated and participate socially and economically as citizens*', recognised the connection between educational fulfilment in care and the quality of life after care. The priority given to this area by the Government was also reflected by the introduction of the performance assessment framework, new Guidance on the education of looked after children, the introduction of Personal Education Plans, and the requirement contained within the Children (Leaving Care) Act 2000 to provide financial assistance and support to young people in education beyond the age of 21.

However, in response to ongoing evidence of poor levels of attainment, the Social Exclusion Unit (SEU), in their 2003 report, *A Better Education for Children in Care*, identified five key reasons why children in care under achieve in education:

- Placement instability.

- Too much time out of school.

- Insufficient help with education.

- Primary carers not being expected or equipped to provide sufficient support and encouragement for learning and development.

- Many children having unmet, emotional, mental and physical health needs.

The SEU report highlighted the evidence that young people in care were nine times more likely to have a Statement of Special Educational Needs than their non-care peers. Recent research has also shown the very high level of mental health, or emotional and behavioural difficulties among looked after children and young people leaving care.[24] The complexity of these mental health issues, and their roots, often lying within children's earlier damaging intra-family relations, and the failure of the care system to compensate young people, highlights the challenge in improving educational attainment, especially when normative measures of educational attainment are used as the main indicator. Some young people may travel a long way just to re-engage with education.

However, there has been no weakening of resolve by the Government. Following a Green Paper consultation process, further proposals are detailed within the White Paper, *Care Matters: Time for Change*, the implementation plan *Care Matters: Time to Deliver for Children in Care*, and legislated for in the Children and Young Persons Act 2008. In the *Care Matters* implementation plan, the role of the 'Virtual

School Head' is seen as pivotal in supporting the work of the 'designated teacher', in improving educational standards, as is the role of CAMHS, and the co-ordination of health services to progress actions identified in children and young people's health plans: 'this is not solely a job for local authority social workers – health services must be proactive corporate parents as well' (p.15).

In respect of improving the experience of children and young people at school, the Children and Young Persons Act 2008 will include: supporting greater educational stability by ensuring that the education of children in care is not disrupted as a result of care placement moves; putting the role of a designated teacher for young people in care on a statutory footing in order to help them overcome barriers to their learning; and ensuring local authorities financially support those who go on to Higher Education.

Other provisions in the Act which are aimed at improving the quality of care, and therefore may impact upon education, are: strengthening the role of the Independent Reviewing Officer, so that the voice of children and young people is central to the planning and review system; placing a specific duty on social workers to visit all looked after children and young people, including those living in children's homes, supported independent accommodation and youth custody; making 'Independent Visitors' available to a wider group of children; extending the duty to appoint a personal adviser and keep pathway planning under regular review, to all care leavers who start or resume a programme of education or training after the age of 21 up until 25, and, also when moving from a stable care placement to an 'independent' flat or hostel; ensuring the continuing supervision of children in long-term residential placements made by education and health services whilst supporting the role of the family; and piloting 'Social Work Practices'.

The detailed proposals contained within *Care Matters: Time to Deliver for Children in Care*, for improving education, are consistent with the main ideas informing the *Children's Plan: Building Brighter Futures*, published in December 2007, in particular, by reaching out to disadvantaged young people through 'personalised' teaching, learning and support, as well as the recognition of emotional and behavioural difficulties, as obstacles to educational progress. The White Paper, *Back on Track*, published in May 2008, details the Government's strategy for modernising alternative educational provision for young people who are permanently excluded from school and those who require specialist help with learning and behavioural difficulties. Furthermore, improving outcomes for children and young people in care is seen as the responsibility of all local partners, led by Directors of Children's Services, including local authorities, Primary Care Trusts, foster carers, residential workers social workers, GPs and other health care practitioners and teachers.

Educating Difficult Adolescents

Educating Difficult Adolescents set out to evaluate the implementation of the educational objectives of *Quality Protects*, focusing specifically on improving educational achievements and reducing permanent exclusions and unauthorised absences, in three contrasting local authorities.[25] There were three main parts to the study:

1. An exploration was carried out of the 'corporate parenting' role, including the development and implementation of policy related to the *Quality Protects* programme. This drew upon local policy documents, interviews with mangers, as well as statistical analysis on the progress of looked after children in the three areas.

2. A detailed follow-up study was done of the care, educational experiences and outcomes of 150 young people who had 'difficulties' – behaviour that was difficult to manage at home school or in the community including: poor school attendance or exclusion; behavioural problems in school; regular use of alcohol or drugs; offending, self-harm, or aggression or violence. These young people were equally divided between groups living in foster care, children's homes and residential schools for pupils presenting 'behavioural, emotional and social difficulties' (BESD formerly known as EBD). This part of the study was derived from semi-structured interviews with young people, carers and teachers, and also included consultations with the *Family Rights Group* and *A National Voice* to enhance service user perspectives.

3. An analysis was carried out of the comprehensive costs of care and education services related to outcomes. The study was undertaken between 2003 and 2006.

What were the main findings? Stage 1 of the study, as detailed above, showed that the attainment of looked after young people (as measured by Key Stage 4; GCSE/GNVQ) in the three local authorities was much lower than for young people in the general school population, although local statistics were often based on small numbers of pupils and could be unreliable. Overall, academic achievements of looked after children fluctuated in the three areas but very few permanent exclusions were recorded.

In Stage 2 of the study, although 150 'difficult adolescents' were recruited to the sample, there were differences in the family backgrounds of those recruited from local authorities and residential schools. The family members of the looked after group were significantly more likely to have serious problems including alcohol and drug misuse, criminal behaviour, mental health difficulties and domestic violence. The young people in this group also were more likely to have been seriously abused and neglected and be separated from their birth parents at an earlier age. The researchers comment:

It is the combination of adversities that brings with it particular stresses. Individual stressful experiences, in themselves, tend to inflict limited damage, but the effects of several are cumulative: looked after young people had worse combinations of family adversities than those recruited from the residential special schools.

There were also important differences between these two groups in how professionals assessed their family links. In almost nine out of every ten of the residential school sample professionals believed that young people would identify their birth family as their 'home base', compared with only half of the local authority group. This is understandable in that to be placed in a residential school young people usually have a stable home base. Also, whereas three-quarters of the schools sample had unrestricted access to their birth family, this dropped to only a third for the looked after group. In helping young people, the researchers found that a wide variety of provision was used, including different types of children's homes and dual-registered homes and schools. Also, three-quarters of young people received some form of special educational need support, mainly as a result of 'statements', and this included nearly all of the residential group of young people.

In terms of placement stability, 40 per cent of the whole sample of difficult adolescents changed placements during the nine-month follow-up period, and ten per cent moved on more than one occasion. Half the moves occurred because the placements broke down, in response to difficult behaviour, or linked to this, to keep the young person out of trouble or safe. Young people living in children's homes were most likely to move and those in the residential group were the most stable, reflecting in part differences in family background, as identified above – those in residential schools having stable family backgrounds. Also, half of the young people who were looked after had a change of social worker over the nine-month follow-up period.

In order to measure the quality of care received by young people during the follow-up period, the researchers developed their own instrument, *A Quality of Care Index*, in the main derived from earlier research studies of residential and foster care. This included nine key areas, each one, for assessment purposes, divided into a number of sub-categories (see Figure 6.1).

The aim of this measure was to present a picture of the whole 'care package', based on researcher rating derived from interviews with young people, carers and social workers. Overall, the researchers judged the quality of care (derived form these nine areas) provided to young people during the nine-month follow-up period to be largely positive. The composite ratings on a four-point scale were: very good (36 per cent); good (45 per cent); fair (17 per cent) and poor (1 per cent). Differences in the quality of care were related to type of placement, the children's home group fared less well than the other groups, although there were differences within this group – 'some homes managed to offer a better care environment, greater security and a wider package of support from others'.

Care and control

- Addressing children's needs/child-oriented.
- Warm and caring/responsive.
- Quality of physical environment.
- Praise and responsibility/positive expectations.
- Opportunities for success/improvement of self-image.
- Clear boundaries/behavioural management.
- Opportunities for inclusion.

Stability and continuity

- Placement changes.
- Pressure to move prematurely/opportunity to remain.
- Changes in caregivers/predictability in daily care.

Safety

- Child protection issues.
- Management of risk, e.g. life-style.
- Peer violence.
- Allegation(s).

Inter-professional working

- Support for identified problems, particularly liaison between placement/school.
- Help with behavioural, emotional and social problems.
- A coherent approach.

Family links

- Encourage contact in a discriminatory way (including siblings).
- Consider young person's views.
- Attempt to obtain support of parents.
- Consider transport issues.

Close relationship with at least one adult

- Champion/advocate/someone to stand up for young person (including professional).
- Support/time to spend with young person.
- Reliability.
- Effectiveness of social worker/educational psychologist role.
- Encouragement of appropriate contact with key adult(s) from the past.

Ethnicity and culture

- Culture/language/and religion.

- Context/location.

- Consideration to ethnic matching/staff mix/role models.

- Daily care.

Friendships

- Encouragement of *pro-social* friends.

Planning and aftercare

- High quality assessment and planning/follow processes.

- Desired placements; choice/matching.

- Young person's involvement/listen to young person.

Figure 6.1 Quality of Care Index

Promoting Quality: The Role of Educational Support Teams

Each of the three authorities operated variants of Education Support Teams (EST). These offered dedicated educational support for looked after children (LAC) – one comprised 25 staff, including advisory teachers and educational psychologists.

Education Support Teams' services included monitoring the overall progress of pupils, such as establishing a system of predicted grades. One EST funded a national call centre, which each morning telephoned schools to see if LAC pupils had arrived. If not, it then contacted the placement to find out the explanation (e.g. illness) and, if necessary, alerted the EST to the absenteeism. They also organised achievement ceremonies to celebrate the attainments of LAC – these were very popular, often attended by local celebrities.

Another important role of Educational Support Teams was to offer training and support to teachers and carers. This included:

- Running multi-agency training.

- Meeting with each new teacher and social worker as part of their induction.

- Organising education-focused summer schools and motivational schemes to encourage Year 12/13 (6th form) study (including cash vouchers).

- Offering a carers' resource centre, which loaned learning resources and provided advice.

> • And supporting carers and Year 11 pupils in the weeks preceding GCSE exams – giving advice on completing coursework, revision strategies, exam skills and dealing with 'exam stress'.
>
> There was also direct support for pupils including: newsletters each term; providing homework support; and helping to prepare home-study timetables and study packs for excluded pupils or those temporarily without a school place.

The researchers also explored the educational progress of young people during the follow-up period. The carers or social workers viewed that about 20 per cent of young people were achieving at the level that would be expected for their age; about 40 per cent were felt to be making good educational progress; just under a third had stayed about the same; and about ten per cent were thought to be deteriorating in their education. Consistent with the discussion above, education for the children's home group was particularly problematic.

Nearly half of the total sample of young people had changed educational provision during the follow-up period, although this was often seen as a positive move. Also, the majority of young people were assessed as making an improvement in a general measure of behavioural, emotional and social difficulties. The researchers found an association between young people's assessment of the quality of care they received and their satisfaction with schooling and general happiness; and that changes of placement were associated with lower levels of general happiness, less satisfaction with school, and to some extent, friendship.

Promoting Quality: Maintaining Stability in Schooling

Chris was in Year 11 (16 years old) and had been living in a foster home in northern England for two months. He liked it there and was living with experienced carers. His social worker said that this was one of the worst cases of neglect the department had seen. There was domestic violence and his father sexually abused Chris's two sisters. Previous foster placements had broken down due to his aggression. He assaulted his foster mother and was charged.

Chris attended the same school that he did prior to this foster placement. This involves an hour's taxi journey each way, which costs £100 a day. The social worker observed: 'School has been the main stable thing – they are an excellent school.' Chris commented: 'I've got used to the journey, I don't mind.'

Chris goes into a learning support centre at school and shares a classroom assistant. An education advisory teacher from the authority goes in to the school to work with him and she chairs his reviews. There are 28 in his class. His social worker thinks he should get the required 3 D grades at GCSE to stay on at school: 'He wouldn't succeed at college, he's too vulnerable.' Foster carers go to parents' evenings. Chris says: 'I think they really want me to do well.'

Finally, as detailed at the beginning of the chapter, the study had an economic component, describing the services and supports used by young people and the costs associated with them. As regards the bigger picture, this showed that local authorities were spending the most money on children and young people with the greatest needs – it was the young people with the most difficulties who were placed in the most expensive facilities. However, the researchers found no evidence to suggest that increased resources were generating improved outcomes – but that those making decisions about placements were allocating resources with regard to the level of difficulties young people have to overcome. More specifically, the analysis of costs revealed little difference between local authorities and that young people accessed a wide range of services during the nine-month follow-up period, including GPs, dentists and opticians. But only a third used mental health services – 'concerning, given that the sample was selected as having behaviours that pose considerable management challenges'.

- Having corporate parenting arrangements in place, including integrated working approaches, to improving the educational outcomes for looked after children and young people.

- Bringing together workers to identify and respond to both the 'care' and 'educational' needs of children and young people.

- Identifying educational difficulties, including Special Educational Needs, when they arise in families and in children and young people's placements.

- Having clear arrangements between schools and children's social care for early interventions.

- Having clear arrangements between schools, CAMHS and children's social care for assisting young people with emotional and behavioural problems.

Figure 6.2 Integrated working: Issues arising from research

Conclusion

This study has focused on the educational objectives of the *Quality Protects* programme, specifically in relation to 'difficult' young people living in children's homes, foster care and residential special schools. The sample included young people with educational problems, as well as those presenting 'behavioural, emotional and social difficulties'. Most were considered to have special educational needs, mainly BESD, and there was clear evidence that this led to additional support and resources to meet their learning needs.

The researchers argue that focusing exclusively on educational outcomes as a measure of progress for this group of 'difficult' young people is limited, as it fails to take into account a young person's family background, as well as the late age many young people enter care, often with entrenched educational problems. This raises the wider and complex issue of how best to prevent children becoming 'difficult adolescents' in the first place. As detailed above, the *Care Matters* agenda and proposals contained within the Children and Young Persons Act 2008 contain a number of key proposals. What is evident is that integrated working between schools, children's social care and health services will be critical to both the preventative and ongoing responsive agendas.

The main issues and implications for policy and practice arising from this study include:

- A wider measure of progress that takes into account a young person's behavioural, emotional and social difficulties should be adopted. For the purpose of their study the researchers developed a *Quality of Care Index* (see Figure 6.1) that covered a wide range of measures, drawing upon the views of the key respondents: young people, carers and professionals.

- Reducing movement and instability; lower turnover of social workers; and more consideration should be given to the role and functioning of the children's home sector.

- Placement categories are not necessarily superior to others. What seems more important are the attributes of the particular individuals with whom the young person lives and the quality of experience that they offer.

- The delivery and impact of wider services are very important, including the school, social work, educational psychology and mental health provision.

Questions for Children's Services
Strategic

- How does your placement commissioning strategy take into account factors which the evidence suggests are likely to lead to better educational, emotional and social outcomes?

- What measures, in addition to national indicators, does your Partnership or Children's Trust use to monitor improvement in educational outcomes for looked after children?

- How does your workforce strategy shape, support and develop the children's workforce, in ways which promote effective common approaches to meeting the needs of looked after children?

- To what extent do your Corporate Parenting arrangements champion and drive integrated working approaches to improving educational outcomes for looked after children?

Operational

- In what ways do your organisational structures and processes promote or impede placement stability, and continuity of the social worker or lead professional?

- How do you know that Personal Education Plans are being used to create effective personalised packages of support engaging the young person, carer, (designated) teacher, social worker and other professionals?

- Is the Personal Education Award being used effectively to support this approach?

- How do you ensure that professionals from across Children's Services are enabled to work together to address care and education needs equally?

Practice

- Could use of a tool such as the *Quality of Care Index*, improve the way in which you match the whole package of care and support to the assessed needs of a child or young person?

- How do you address the needs of young people with behavioural, emotional and social difficulties (BESD), including access to CAMHS, and how do you support their carers?

- What additional intensive support is made available for looked after children to support their learning needs alongside their emotional needs?

- How well equipped are young people, carers and relevant professionals to contribute to and engage with Personal Education Plans and how could this be improved?

Chapter 7

Advocating and Participating

It's a bit like we get involved for a week or a month but then it peters out until the next time they want us.

(Young disabled person's view of being consulted about services)

A lot of the young people expect you to do the work for them, but we worked on this together. He came in and we did the letter together at the computer … I felt quite proud of that case because he did a lot of the work himself.

(Advocate)

We should encourage all organisations to put the voice of the child at the heart of what they do – the dream is that we won't need advocacy.

(Manager, Children's Services)

Introduction

The participation of children and young people in decisions that affect their lives is a central platform of current government policy. But its roots go back over 30 years, to the Children Act 1975, which for the first time, placed a duty on local authorities *'to ascertain as far as is practicable the wishes and feelings of the child and give due consideration to them, having regard to his age and understanding'* (Section 59). This was the beginning of a journey that has seen major developments in law, policy and practice.

Both the Children Acts of 1980 and 1989 required local authorities to ascertain the *'wishes and feelings'* of children they look after, or are about to look after, thus providing the legal framework for an emerging rights movement of children in care, as well as much innovatory practice. The Government's ratification of the United Nations Convention on the Rights of the Child in 1991, recognised children's rights to expression and to receiving information, and this was reinforced by Article 10 of the 1998 Human Rights Act.

Also, as detailed in Chapter 1, children's participation is central to the *Quality Protects* programme, launched in 1998. But it is an ongoing journey – the *Every*

Child Matters agenda, the Children Act 2004, the role of the Children's Commissioner, the National Service Framework for Young People and Maternity Services and the Children's Plan all recognise the importance of children's participation. In *Care Matters: Time to Deliver for Children in Care*, the 'voice of the child', is identified as a foundation of 'excellent corporate parenting', alongside 'high aspirations' and 'stable relationships'. Good practice examples of participation, included within the *Care Matters* implementation plan, include developing a Pledge to all young people who are in or leaving care and the setting up of Children in Care Councils. In addition to strengthening the role of Independent Reviewing Officers, in the Children and Young Persons Act 2008 (as discussed in Chapter 2), advocacy, is also identified in the *Care Matters* implementation plan as having an important role to play.

Thinking about participation, including advocacy, has also been part of this journey. Is it about children and young people being informed about decisions that affect them, being present when decisions are made, being represented at decision-making bodies, being involved themselves, being consulted, being influential, or taking decisions themselves? In exploring these questions, Arnstein, nearly 40 years ago, proposed her classic ladder of participation in relation to citizen involvement and this has been much adapted and drawn on by others for children's participation.[26]

In similar vein, the distinction has been made between 'active' advocacy, where children speak for themselves, or where this is seen as the purpose of advocacy, and 'passive advocacy', where the advocate speaks on behalf of the child. However, more recently, it has been recognised that children's participation will depend upon age, capability and choice of the child, as well as the type of decisions to be taken. In this context, Kirby *et al.* (2003) have proposed a non-hierarchical model in which the type of activity will be linked to the situation, and which recognises that participation is a process, not a single event.[27]

The 'thinking' about participation has also included the arguments put forward for children and young people's participation and the foundation of a rights-based approach to Children's Services: to uphold children's rights; to fulfil legal responsibilities; to improve services; to improve decision-making; to enhance the democratic process; and to promote children's protection. But far less thought has gone into exploring the murky waters: who participates, and why, who doesn't, and why, how far are children's views shaped and used by adults for their own ends? Also, given the appeal and popularity of participation, there is a notable lack of descriptive and evaluative research. Two connected studies included in this overview were commissioned to increase our knowledge of this area. The first study, the *Participation* study, aimed to improve our understanding of the participation of disabled children and young people, and the second, the *Advocacy* study, the role of advocacy in facilitating the participation of looked after children and children in need in decision-making.

The participation of disabled children and young people

Aiming High for Disabled Children: Better Support for Families (2007) identifies *access and empowerment* as a priority area to improve outcomes for disabled children:

> Empowering disabled young people and their families means: improved provision of information and greater transparency in decision-making … putting families in control of the design and delivery of their care packages and services … and supporting disabled children and young people and their parents to shape services. (pp.15–16)

Earlier material, aimed at enhancing the involvement of children, developed for the *Integrated Children's System* website, also included disabled children.

A review of the research literature suggests that whilst children and young people are increasingly being involved in decision-making, this has been slower for disabled children. Also, less is known about the specific factors which can promote disabled children's participation, in comparison to other children.[28] In this context, the *Participation* study investigated disabled children and young people's participation within decision-making, to identify factors which can support and promote good practice in terms of the process and outcomes of participation. It had a particular focus on children with complex needs, those young people who were seen as 'hard to reach', including those young people with communication impairments, autistic spectrum disorders or complex health needs.

The study, carried out between 2003 and 2005, had three stages: first an analysis of Management Action Plans (MAPs) to identify participation work with disabled children and provide a summary of the range and types of participation; second, a survey of all Social Services departments in England to identify and describe ongoing work (information received from 71 local authorities, 70 per cent response rate); and third, case studies of participation activity in six areas, to explore in more depth the processes and outcomes of participation. In the case studies interviews were carried out with 21 disabled children, aged five to 18, 24 parents including carers and 76 professionals.

Survey findings

The first part of the study, the analysis of the MAPs, showed 'little depth and clarity' about participation work, and the information gathered was also very dated, by the time the research was due to be carried out. It was therefore decided to survey all Social Services departments. The main results from the survey of social service departments showed that 60 per cent involved disabled children in both service development and decision-making regarding their own care, and 40 per cent indicated involvement in just one of these processes. In relation to decisions regarding their own care, they were more likely to be involved in their own reviews and least likely to be involved within child protection conferences or their own health plans. As regards service development, they were most likely to be consulted about play or leisure services.

The survey also showed a wide variation in the numbers of disabled children involved in participation between different areas – from less than 10 to over 50. Young people were likely to participate in decisions about their care from age 11, peaking at around the age of 14–16. The survey response also showed that the participation of young people described as 'difficult to reach' was growing, and children and young people with communication impairments, degenerative conditions, autistic spectrum disorders and complex needs were participating in the majority of authorities.

Dedicated funding to promote disabled children's involvement in tailoring individual packages of care also varied. Just over a half of authorities reported that they had funding and most of these had benefited from *Quality Protects* which had been used to fund advocacy workers, children's rights officers, and some participation workers, often through voluntary sector agencies. *Quality Protects* funding, as well as other sources, were used to fund initiatives focused on children's participation in service development. Eighty per cent of these initiatives involved partnership working and under a half (44 per cent) involved the voluntary sector. The other main partners included education authorities (27 per cent), health, Primary Care Trusts and NHS Trusts (30 per cent) and schools and colleges (11 per cent).

The authorities surveyed used a wide variety of methods to involve disabled children and young people. This included the development of their own materials, existing published resources, as well as written verbal, computer and creative arts-based methods.

Promoting Quality: 'Choice Making' Through the Production of an Interactive DVD

An authority worked in partnership with a multi-media company and regional dance development agency, to provide disabled children and young people with creative opportunities to express themselves and produce an interactive DVD. Over 30 children with severe learning difficulties, physical impairments and/or those who use non-verbal communications systems were involved in workshops or worked one-to-one with two artists. The aim was to provide material for the DVD, and give participants opportunities to access art, drama, music, animation and multi-media techniques to facilitate choice-making.

The purpose of the DVD was to provide disabled young people, who may be coming into a residential unit for an extended stay or respite care, with information on what to expect and what it might be like.

The DVD produced contained an interactive game for children which followed a child through a day. At each juncture of the day, e.g. getting up, having breakfast, watching TV, the viewer is required to make a choice. The commentator describes the options, subtitles and Makaton symbols are also shown, different choices lead into another part of the story. The game relays the message that disabled children have choices, should be given choices in their everyday life, should be encouraged to develop their skills and experience to make choices and that choices have consequences.

Children act as some of the main characters in the DVD. The film producers, wherever possible, encouraged the children to make choices and influence the content and direction of the film.

Alongside the interactive game, there is a documentary where professionals and staff from respite units explain how disabled children are encouraged during their stay to develop their communication and decision-making skills, and the importance this has for children. It also tries to paint a realistic picture about balancing choice with practical implications, namely, that choice is not always available and may sometimes be denied, for example, if there are safety issues.

The survey also showed that most authorities provided support for children to facilitate their involvement, although the comments suggested this could be minimal and variable. Also, although advocacy services were widely available, there were low levels of training for children and young people and little information about decision-making processes. Training for staff centred mainly on communication and its related methods, often accessed through voluntary agencies. Not all young people involved in participation were provided with feedback about decisions made about their own care or about service development.

Case studies

The case studies in the six areas provided an opportunity to explore in more depth the experiences of disabled children, their parents and carers, and the professionals involved in assisting them. Two of the areas focused on involving children in decisions about their own care through the review process; three of the areas were concerned with participation activities which involved children and young people in service developments; and one area carried out both types of activity.

The case study analysis showed that only small numbers of children were involved in decisions about their own care and there was little evidence of partnership working. However, many of the social workers and parents or carers interviewed spoke of the need for working with those who were expert in communication methods and saw the benefit of working more closely with schools and education – they were often unaware of techniques and systems being used within schools and lacked the skills in using the child's communication method:

Going into school, where the school has the child for however many hours per day and gets to know that child very, very well and obviously begins to understand their communication system. I often feel I would like to have more time to spend within a school situation learning from the people with that child, that would be really, really helpful. (Social Work Practitioner)

The study found a reported need for more information sharing and, in particular, greater partnerships between schools, parents and carers, social workers and the wider network of professionals working with disabled children around communication methods.

As regards service development, two types of activity were organised, large-scale participation activity days and youth forums and advisory groups. Whereas the former were able to involve larger numbers of disabled children, there were sometimes restricted opportunities for children to express their views about services – which was more likely to be achieved by the youth forums. However, both were successful in providing young people with new experiences, although participants were likely to be older young people, and there was limited involvement of children with complex needs.

Promoting Quality: A Child-Centred Approach to Review Meetings of Short Stays for Disabled Children and Young People

An authority undertook a pilot project to facilitate disabled children's involvement, including children with communication impairments, learning difficulties and/or complex needs.

An audio photo invitation card was sent to invite children to their review of short stays. This attempted to make it clear that the child was the central focus. Social workers recorded a brief message which played each time the card was opened. The card contained photographs of a typical meeting and of the social worker and child. Also included were instructions on how a child could record a reply if they want to.

A 'review pack' was developed, containing questions about aspects of the service, photographs to place the questions in context and 'feelings faces' on a scale of 'happy', 'ok' and 'sad' so that children could indicate their level of satisfaction through whichever communication method they preferred. For some, the feeling faces were not appropriate; social workers then showed children the photographs and recorded their response whether that was facial expression, gesture or body language.

The review meeting was restructured to be more child-centred. A first meeting was held between parents, social worker and chair to discuss any lengthy or contentious issues which might preclude a child taking part. Then the social worker met the child and gathered their views via the review pack. The final stage was the actual review, where the social worker and child would feedback the child's views and discuss issues arising from the initial meetings. Because of the prior meetings, the review meeting was shorter and could be governed by the amount of time the child was able or willing to participate.

Social workers attended a training session where the new format of meetings, review pack and rationale were explained. They were also given guidance on different communication methods. The authority intended to expand this successful pilot.

Professional staff were, some of the time, unclear about the aims and possibilities of participation, especially for children with communication difficulties and learning impairments. They expressed concerns about competence, understanding and ability to participate, as well as the problems of interpreting children's views. Also, some workers believed that participation was invalid unless it involves children and young people taking part in review meetings and contributing to complex decision-making processes. Some parents also had concerns about their child's potential to participate, or the social worker's ability to assist the child. But, there was also evidence that both parents and professionals changed their views as a consequence of children's experience, reflecting that they had underestimated their potential.

Advocacy for looked after children and children in need

In *Care Matters: Time to Deliver for Children in Care*, advocacy is seen as having 'an important role to play in ensuring children's voices are heard and their rights protected, especially where they intend to make a complaint' (p.8).

A 2008 report by the Children's Rights Director for England, *Children's Views on Advocacy*, showed that children and young people who had experience of advocacy had very positive experiences of advocates, in listening, putting over their point of view, getting others to listen to them, and respecting their privacy. Nine out of ten children and young people said that their advocates had either made a difference for them, or had sometimes made a difference. However, of the 138 young people who gave their views, only just over a half had heard of advocacy, and one in five did not know how to get an advocate. Many children and young people did get help from others, but didn't have a clear view of what counts as advocacy.[29]

A review of the literature, carried out to inform the development of the *Advocacy* study, identified a number of gaps in knowledge that the study was designed to address: the need to describe the range of advocacy services and the methods used by advocates to work with children of different ages and capacities; the need for more information on the relationship between individual advocacy and broader participation strategies; the need to have an understanding of advocacy from the perspectives of the different groups, and how advocates manage competing views between parents, carers, professionals and children and young people; and, finally, the need for evidence on the impact of advocacy.[30]

In exploring these issues the research was carried out in two stages. First, a telephone survey of 75 advocacy services for children and young people in England was completed (77 per cent response rate). Second, an in-depth qualitative study of ten advocacy services for children and young people was carried out, including five specialist services: a secure juvenile justice setting; a secure psychiatric setting; child protection; disabled children and young people; looked after children. A further five advocacy services were selected because they engaged with a wider range of children and young people: those 'in need', children with disabilities, young people leaving care, very young children, teenagers and black and minority ethnic young people. Interviews were carried out with 48 children and young people, 13 parents and carers, 18 advocates, and 40 health and social care professionals. The study was carried out between 2003 and 2005.

What were the main findings? First, the research showed the wide variation in the availability of advocacy services between different geographical areas, as well as differences in the groups of children and young people targeted by advocacy services. Access to advocacy support could be related to age, disability, type of placement, and asylum status in some services but not others. The telephone survey found that the great majority of advocacy services had some contact with services other than social services: education was the most commonly cited, followed by health services, mental health services and youth justice. Education services were most likely to be described as 'difficult to work with', whilst social services were most likely to be described as 'relatively easy':

> I think that social services are the easiest, because they have an understanding of advocacy from the outset. We often find education difficult to engage with, particularly secondary schools. (Advocacy service respondent)

The survey found that advocacy services used various forms of publicity, as a means of contacting children and young people, including newsletters, leaflets, posters, information packs, and these were directed at schools, health centres, libraries, youth clubs, pubs and fast food outlets. As regards the 'most common reasons' why young people ask advocates for help, the research found, in descending order (percentages add up to more than 100 per cent as respondents were asked to cite the three most common reasons): placement issues (48 per cent); not being listened to (25 per cent); problems with social workers (24 per cent); financial and accommodation issues for care leavers (24 per cent); support at reviews and other meetings (23 per cent); contact issues with families and siblings (23 per cent); complaints (17 per cent); inadequate care planning (16 per cent); financial issues for looked after children (15 per cent); and education (12 per cent), including helping young people to attend schools and further education colleges of their choice.

Second, the study found that some local authorities had developed a culture of listening to children and young people including support for advocacy, although this was uneven. The researchers suggest 'individual advocacy is likely to have the greatest impact on Children's Services where it operates in synergy with broader participation strategies'. The study also showed that advocacy services also worked with young people who had multiple problems and therefore involvement of a number of Children's Services, including education and health.

Promoting Quality: Advocacy Practice

A key issue for advocacy practice concerns the ways in which advocates intervene where there are differences of opinion, or potential conflicts of interest, between children and their parents or carers. The literature review highlighted a twin and contradictory trend towards the greater acceptance of consulting children about their care, and an increasing emphasis upon parental rights and authority. However, little evidence was identified that described how advocates engage with, and resolve, conflicts of interest between children and their parents or carers.

Findings from our study indicated that such tensions are most likely to emerge in relation to children involved in child protection processes, and disabled children. However, looked after children also engage with this problem – for example, when they attempt to negotiate contact arrangements with family members. For example, in the following case, we see that all participants have their views – the parent, the foster carer, the young person and the social worker. However, in the face of several and potentially competing adult views, Noreen expresses the need for an advocate to help her 'have a voice' in this situation and to be heard.

'I wanted help because I was struggling at school because the relationship with my foster carer was failing … (there were) lots of arguments about contact with my real mum … (the advocate) was there to encourage me, help me say what I needed to say and support me. Sometimes she spoke out. The social worker listened to what me and the advocate had to say, and sorted out proper routine contact with Mum, no arguments. Mum wasn't really happy because contact had got less, but she was happy that the arguments had stopped, because we knew where we stood.' (Noreen, 14 years)

The advocate helps Noreen to speak up for herself and, when Noreen struggles to express her views, to speak on her behalf. The social worker appears to have the capacity to genuinely listen to Noreen and her advocate, and to take their views seriously. On the basis of this information, the social worker reached a compromise between the foster parent, the biological parent and Noreen which, whilst it did not entirely satisfy the parent, nonetheless was acceptable to all parties. As a consequence, the negative effects of repeated and unresolved conflict on Noreen's emotional well-being were reduced. An unanticipated outcome was that Noreen's progress at school improved.

Third, the *Advocacy* research showed that formal complaints processes were widely seen by advocates and social care workers as an inappropriate and ineffective way of resolving concerns raised by young people. Resolving complaints informally and at an earlier stage was seen as more effective, and formal complaints procedures were seen by both advocates and social care staff as less accessible to young children, disabled children, those engaged in child protection processes and those seeking asylum. Fourth, the study also identified gaps in the training, support and funding of advocacy services. They also found that funding impacted upon most aspects of service organisation and delivery, and that single-worker services suffered from isolation, stress and inadequate resources, in terms of time and skills to provide a service that is inclusive of different needs.

Promoting Quality: The Impact of Advocacy

Our study sought to explore evidence for the impact of advocacy at two levels: (a) on the individual lives of looked after children, and children in need, and (b) on strategic developments in Children's Services. Advocates, social care professionals, parents and carers, and young people themselves identified a wide range of perceived practical and psychological benefits of advocacy for children, including enhanced self-esteem, increased self-confidence and communication skills, improved care packages, the reversal of decisions not perceived to be in the interest of young people's wishes or welfare, and better access to needed services. Most social care professionals and advocates also agreed that a range of policy initiatives could be partly or wholly attributable to advocacy, including: improved financial support for care leavers; changes to incentive schemes for children in secure units; more relaxed procedures on overnight stays; the development of guidelines for supporting looked after young people admitted to hospital; training for foster carers to raise awareness of the effects of treating looked after children differently from the carer's own children; suspension of leaving care reviews when young people sat their GCSEs.

However, just over a fifth of advocates were also frustrated by local authorities' resistance to learning from the lessons of individual advocacy, and applying them to Children's Services on a strategic level. The organisational culture of the local authority emerged as a key factor in either maximising or limiting the potentially positive impact of advocacy for children and young people. For example, one advocacy service was commissioned to offer advocacy support to looked after children in two different local authorities. In one local authority, social care professionals were reported by the advocacy service manager as demonstrating more awareness of the advocacy role, as respecting the independence of the advocacy service, and as more receptive to listening to children's views. By contrast, the relationship between the advocacy service and social care professionals in the second local authority was characterised by conflict and suspicion: 'It's very different and the relationship is more conflict-based because their commitment to children's rights and advocacy isn't there ...' (Shaheen, advocacy service manager).

Barriers to achieving better outcomes for children were identified as an over-reliance on the part of social care professionals on bureaucratic procedures, and professional resistance to young people's participation in decision-making. The local authority that was more receptive to children's participation in decisions about their care used individual advocacy casework as a form of internal audit to introduce strategic improvements to services for looked after children.

'We work in two local authorities and in one of these we have had a big input into service development, particularly where the Leaving Care Team is concerned. There have also been other changes – on overnight stays, and police checks on friends, and an increase in the Leaving Care Grant. In the other authority, it's difficult to tell' (Shaheen, advocacy service manager).

'We've moved from being an organisation that met our needs to one that met young people's needs' (Gilly, manager, Children's Services).

Finally, as regards the impact of advocacy, in addition to the areas identified in the above example the study showed that advocates play an important role in facilitating children's access to services. Examples cited by advocates included: access to GP services and drug rehabilitation services; helping children and young people obtain better health care, such as support for dealing with self-harm, and sexual health advice; access to services for single parents – Sure Start programmes and playgroup facilities; access to leisure facilities – football training, obtaining free swimming passes, referrals to youth clubs; and, as detailed above, access to education and training.

- Identifying in your Children and Young People's Plan the contribution of advocacy services and the commitment to participation, across all services including education, children's social care and health settings.

- Having arrangements for joint working with schools on the communication methods of disabled children.

- Directing information about advocacy services at schools, health centres, youth centres and other venues where young people meet.

Figure 7.1 Integrated working: issues arising from research

Conclusion

The *Participation* study suggested that participation among disabled children and young people could be increased in a number of ways:

- By having a shared understanding of the aims and objectives of participation among all those involved – children and young people, professionals and parents.

- By the provision of more training, resources and support for staff. Reported needs included: communication methods, IT, and creative skills to develop and adapt participation methods. The study also identified a need for training in the theory and methods of participation with particular focus on disabled children and young people. As regards resources, many workers felt that there should be more recognition of the time needed to undertake participation work.

- By embedding participation activity within the culture of organisations. This would help protect against participation, whether in individual decisions or service events, being one-off events. The researchers note the 'fragility and fragmented nature of participation activity' – much practice rested on a few key dedicated professionals and was isolated from other activities.

- By the identification of who is best placed to communicate with disabled children, joint working with schools, information sharing on preferred communication methods, and by the details of each child's method of communication being recorded on case files.

- By more systematic procedures for recording, monitoring and evaluating participation activities. The case studies showed that when participation did happen, children, parents and professional staff all reported positive effects, including feeling valued, being listened to, gaining confidence, learning new skills and having lots of fun. Parents valued learning about their children's views. There is also a need to systematically provide feedback to children and young people.

The main implications for policy and practice arising out of the *Advocacy* study were:

- Policy-makers should work towards greater consistency and equity in children's access to advocacy support. Reciprocal arrangements between existing advocacy services can improve access for children in out-of-area placements and residential settings.

- Those responsible for children's social services should provide information on advocacy services as soon as they enter care, before they attend reviews, at the initial stage of the complaints procedure, and before involvement in the child protection process.

- Advocacy services need more diverse methods for disseminating information about their work, especially using different media, direct work and the use of IT. Information should be directed at schools, health centres, youth centres and other venues where young people meet. Also, sharing of good practice, especially in relation to diversity, and recruiting advocates from different backgrounds, may contribute to improved access.

- Support is provided for both individual advocacy and broader participation strategies to enable children and young people to 'have a voice' in the development of Children's Services. This may be helped by providing information on the role of advocates in initial and in-service training of foster carers and social care staff.

- Mechanisms are established to use advocacy as a form of internal audit, to collect information on trends in advocacy services and use this information to contribute to strategic policy developments in Children's Services.

- The role of advocacy services is monitored to ensure that it continues to offer an informal as well a formal service, for addressing problems and resolving complaints.

- Accredited training courses and the introduction of a core curriculum should be introduced.

Questions for Children's Services
Strategic

- Does your Children and Young People's Plan show that disabled children's participation is valued equally across all Children's Services, including children's social care, schools and health settings?

- How do you know that all disabled children and young people have as full a role as possible in service development, including funding to support disabled children and young people's involvement in tailoring individual packages of care?

- How do you know that your complaints and representations procedures are accessed by children and young people and that the advocacy services in your area are sufficiently well resourced to meet assessed need?

- How would you recognise that your organisation takes full and equal account of the views of children and young people, for example, by monitoring the effectiveness of participation activity?

Operational

- How do you ensure (a) that children and young people are given feedback on what has happened or what will happen as a result of their participation, and (b) that this feedback is provided in ways appropriate to a child's ability and level of comprehension?

- How do you tackle the barriers to embedding participation in the culture and practice of your organisation?

- What do you do to train, support and guide your staff in enabling the full participation of disabled children and young people in service delivery?

- What do you do to ensure that lessons are learned from individual episodes of advocacy and what do you do to apply that learning in future?

- What do you do to ensure that appropriate processes, both informal and formal, are available for the resolution of complaints?

Practice

- How do you identify who is best placed to communicate with disabled children and young people?

- What arrangements do you have for joint working with schools and information sharing on preferred communication methods?

- What do you do to enable disabled children and young people to take part in decision-making and make choices in their everyday lives?

- How do you engage children and young people in the planning and design of services, and how do you challenge negative attitudes to disabled children's participation?

- What do you do to enable and support children and young people in accessing advocacy services?

Chapter 8

Quality Matters in Children's Services

Introduction

Quality is a much used but little defined term. In relation to families, for example, we hear a lot about 'spending quality time with children', or the 'provision of quality child care', but far less about what this means, and to whom – after all, parents, children and those providing Children's Services may view and experience 'quality' very differently. And if you are served an inedible meal at a restaurant, it won't mean very much to be told, when you complain, as I did recently in Leeds, that 'it meets the catering industries quality specification 3065749218 … see the small print at the bottom of the menu, love'. Without an understanding of the concept of quality, and its translation into a working definition or model, it will be difficult to even begin to recognise, or to assess, whether 'quality' services have been provided.

Ten years ago, *Modernising Social Services* (1998) identified two barriers to raising service quality. The first was the gap between social care objectives and the actual standards attained, and the second, whether standards were being achieved consistently. At the same time, *A First Class Service: Quality in the NHS* (1998) highlighted the importance of improving quality in the health services. Building on this foundation, the National Service Frameworks in England were developed, identifying national standards for specific services, including performance indicators against which progress can be measured, both nationally and locally. Also, in 1998, within Children's Services, as detailed in Chapter 1, the *Quality Protects* programme was launched, to improve the quality of services to children in need and those looked after by local authorities.

Quality Protects can be seen as providing a coherent approach to quality development in Children's Services (Figure 8.1). Through the different components it brought together central and local government, involved children, young people and families through the Management Action Plan consultation process, engaged a corporate approach through the involvement of councillors and Chief Executives, provided for leadership at a local and regional level, introduced additional 'special grant' funding and staff support for developing services, and, finally, included a linked research initiative to inform policy and practice.

The main themes arising from the key policy developments, since the introduction of *Quality Protects*, as outlined in Chapter 1 and subsequent chapters, can be seen as providing a policy framework for the development of quality services (see Figure 1.1): Combating social exclusion; universal aspirations and improving outcomes for children in care and their families; multi-agency partnerships and integrated working; personalisation; early intervention and family support; corporate parenting; and empowering users.

Programme Component	Quality Development
National Objectives	Identifies key objectives as a focus for improving the quality and consistency of Children's Services
Performance Indicators	Linked to national objectives, drawn from the Performance Assessment Framework and additional *QP* indicators. Provides transparent criteria against which services can be evaluated and local authorities can measure their performance
Management Action Plans	Local authorities identify deficiencies in services and proposals to overcome these, linked to national objectives and indicators. MAPs progress reports to review existing indicators and develop future indicators
Payment of Special Grant	Funding allocated in response to proposals identified in Management Action Plans, targeted on improvement in specific service areas: supply of adoptive, foster and residential placements; leaving care; disabled children; children's views; assessment planning and records; management information and quality assurance systems
Corporate Ownership and Parenting	Key role for Chief Executive, senior officers, councillors
QP Policy Development	DH Project teams and regional development workers, linking with dedicated local staff
Research Initiative	Nine studies relating to five of the National Objectives. Exploring and evaluating services, and making recommendations to improve the quality of services

Figure 8.1 Quality Protects and quality development in Children's Services

The earlier chapters contain specific recommendations arising out of the findings of the Overview research studies. These identify key policy and practice issues for improving the quality of services in relation to the broad *Quality Protects* objectives under which they have been grouped: ensuring stability; protecting children from abuse and neglect; improving the life chances of looked after children and young people; and involving users in services. In addition, each chapter identifies 'questions for Children's Services', at three levels: the *strategic level*, including those responsible for directing and commissioning services; the *operational level*, including senior managers and heads of services; and the *practice level*, including front-line Children's Services staff and their managers. These can be viewed as 'three levels of quality', and therefore a comprehensive approach to improving quality in Children's Services suggests that action will be required at all three levels, as well as achieving consistency between them.

As will now be evident to the reader, the overview contains a very diverse set of studies – and in this sense it cannot conclude, like its predecessors, with a cumulative distillation of knowledge of a specific form of care, such as foster care, or activity, such as child protection. However, in this concluding chapter, I will also bring together those findings and ideas that either go across the studies, or have wider implications, for the development of quality services. These will be organised around four main themes: what should quality Children's Services aim to provide?; the quality of care and well-being; social work practice and quality services; and making quality happen.

What should quality Children's Services aim to provide?
Stability?

Five of the Overview studies were grouped under Objective 1 of *Quality Protects*, 'ensuring more stability'. These studies show that Children's Services play different roles in relation to different groups of children and young people. The care system, for example, may return children home, or provide short-term supported care, place them with kinship carers or for adoption, provide for their care and upbringing in foster or residential care, and equip them for their journey to adulthood. Planned movement is an important part of the assessment and planning process – so children and young people are able to move as soon as possible to a placement that will meet their needs. The Overview studies also suggest that children and young people should not linger in, or return to, poor quality placements, whether with their family, kinship carers, foster carers, children's homes or residential schools. In that sense, stability, as a generalised aim of quality services, is by itself, limited, and, in recognition of this, several of the Overview studies included measures of well-being in their research design.

Well-being?

Well-being has been conceptualised in different ways.[31] In the international research literature this has included measures of physical well-being (including mortality, morbidity, accidents, diet, physical abuse and neglect); cognitive well-being (including educational development and attainment); behavioural well-being (including offending behaviour, drug, alcohol and substance abuse) and emotional well-being (including mental illness, happiness and self-esteem). Also, globally, the United Nations Convention on the Rights of the Child, in its 54 articles, covers 'rights' to survival, development, protection and participation, and in doing so, has been regarded as providing an international framework for examining, and nations being accountable for, the well-being of their children and young people.

In England, as detailed in Chapter 1, the *Every Child Matters* universal outcomes framework identifies five broad domains of well-being:

- **Economic well-being** – having sufficient income to be able to take advantage of opportunities.

- **Being healthy** – good physical and mental health and living a healthy lifestyle.

- **Staying safe** – being protected from harm and neglect.

- **Enjoying and achieving** – getting the most out of life and developing the skills for adulthood.

- **Making a positive contribution** – having the skills and attitudes to contribute to society.

How these came about is important. They were derived from discussions with children and young people, parents and carers, and professionals working with children, and can be seen as reflecting both a contemporary vision of childhood, which includes both *well-being* and *well-becoming*, and an integrative or multi-agency approach to professional intervention.

Well-being and the 'welfare of children in need'

Most families provide the care and upbringing necessary for the well-being of their children and young people – laying the essential foundation for the five *Every Child Matters* outcomes. However, some parents may experience difficulties and problems which impact upon their capacity to meet the developmental needs of their children and young people. In these circumstances, the Children Act 1989 – subsequently strengthened and modernised by legislation and policy detailed in Chapter 1 – lays out the duties and responsibilities of local authorities and the courts to safeguard and promote 'the welfare of children in need'. As the Overview studies show, these children may have different pathways: they may remain with their parents, helped by the provision of support services; become adopted; go to kinship care, become and remain 'looked after', in foster and residential care; be reunified with their families, or move on to live independent lives. As detailed below, the assessment process is critical to providing appropriate and effective interventions for these vulnerable children and young people. The application of the *Assessment Framework* locates these children and young people's developmental needs within the context of the family and wider community, and as such it is a key connecting process between the 'welfare of children' and the five *Every Child Matters* outcomes, securing their well-being and well-becoming in the future (see Figure 8.2).

Measuring well-being

Five of the studies included in this overview adopted outcome measures covering different dimensions of well-being (*The Pursuit of Permanence; Keeping Them in the Family; The Reunification Study; Kinship Care; Educating Difficult Adolescents*). Of the remaining studies, the *Participation* and *Advocacy* studies highlight the importance of involving children and young people in decision-making processes at both an individual and policy level, and supporting them in this process. Both the *Child Protection* and *Support Foster Care* studies, although not using outcome measures, remind us of the importance of how working with, and supporting parents is closely associated with the well-being of children and young people. What emerges from the nine Overview research studies is a composite or general view of the well-being of children and young people, derived from seven areas:

- Health and development.
- Behaviour.
- Attachment.
- Stability.
- Education and careers.
- Protection.
- Participation.

The assessment of the well-being of children and young people in these studies has been arrived at from a number of different sources including interviews with children and young people, social worker and key worker assessments, standardised measures of well-being (Strengths and Difficulties Questionnaire), case file analysis, or, usually, some combination of these methods. In this regard they represent a summation of views and judgements, or an all-round view, of children and young people's well-being.

But how do children and young people view their well-being? In *Educating Difficult Adolescents* (Chapter 6), the researchers also set out to find out young people's 'sense of well-being', based on their views and feelings. They were asked to complete a series of six ladders, reflecting on different aspects of their lives: school; friendships; relationships with family; happiness in general; staying out of trouble; and achieving their set goals. In each area they were asked to indicate their view on the ladder, with the lowest rung (1) suggesting things were 'as bad as could be', and the top rung (10), 'as good as it could be'. Young people completed these at first and final interview.

Consistent with other research in this area, this exploration of young people's broader sense of well-being, confirmed that many young people can and do find satisfaction in many areas of their lives, despite their often very troubled backgrounds. In this respect their views are often more optimistic than professional assessments of their well-being. More specifically, when the relationship between young people's ratings were explored in relation to other explanatory variables (including quality of care; educational progress; change of placement; personal characteristics), changes of placement were associated with lower levels of general happiness, less satisfaction with the school experience and, to some extent, friendships. Young people's general happiness and satisfaction with schooling were also associated with their perceptions of the quality of care they received – the higher ratings by young people on the rungs of the ladders were recorded where quality of care was rated as 'very good'. As discussed below (Making quality happen), young people's views are central to identifying the quality of services that will enhance their well-being.

Resilience?

As detailed in Chapter 1, there has been increased recognition of the contribution of *resilience* to an understanding of vulnerable children, young people and families. It appeals in a number of ways: first, in its optimism – the evidence of young people doing well in adversity – against all the odds; second, in offering a working framework of 'risk' and 'protective' factors that can provide a clear focus for policy and practice interventions; and third, in giving expression to a 'strength-based' practice in Children's Services, which also provides the platform for participatory and rights-based approaches. Recent research on resilience, funded by the Economic and Social Research Council (ESRC), has underlined the importance of an ecological perspective, recognising the interaction between individual development and context, including social and economic factors – such as poverty and deprivation, family environment and community resources.[32]

Building resilience in children and families is also a central platform of current Government policy, as detailed in *Aiming High for Children: Supporting Families, Aiming High for Disabled Children: Better Support for Families* and the *Care Matters* White Paper. *Aiming High for Children*, in promoting the *Every Child Matters* outcomes, identifies three key 'protective factors' which universal services for children and families are ideally placed to influence: high educational attainment; good social and emotional skills; and positive parenting. It is recognised that these three areas are inter-related and reinforcing, and that there will be specific challenges in reaching and assisting the most disadvantaged children and families – those who in the main are included in the Overview studies.

In this context, the findings, recommendations and 'questions for Children's Services', from the Overview studies are timely, and provide an evidence base that fits well with main proposals contained within theses two papers. *Aiming High for Children*, in addition to *building resilience* includes: *greater personalisation* – that services provided are more responsive to the needs of families, that they offer further support earlier and that packages of support are tailored in accordance with need; *proactive support for those who need it most* – users are engaged and empowered to participate actively in the design and delivery of services, and services need to ensure that they reach out to those children and families who need them most; and *helping families to break out of a cycle of low achievement.*

Aiming High for Disabled Children identifies three priority areas to improve outcomes for disabled children: *access and empowerment* – through the engagement of disabled children and young people in the shaping of services at a local level; *responsive services and timely support* – services which are easily accessible at key transition points, designed around the child and family, and delivered in a co-ordinated and timely manner; and *improving quality* of the services that are particularly vital to improving outcomes for disabled children, young people and families.

To return to the question at the beginning of this section, quality Children's Services should aim to enhance the *well-being* of children, young people and families. The Overview studies have used different but closely related measures, and a composite view of the seven main areas is detailed above. These could also be seen as promoting resilience, in that being described as 'resilient' doesn't mean very much, unless it is related to desired states or defined outcome areas. After all, none of us are completely resilient, in all parts of our lives, all of the time! In terms of the wider policy and practice context, these seven measures also connect with the *Every Child Matters* outcomes framework and dimensions drawn from the *Assessment Framework*, the latter, as detailed above, a pivotal process in identifying effective interventions for vulnerable children and young people (see Figure 8.2).

Every Child Matters	Assessment Framework	Well-being Measures
Economic well-being	Employment, income, housing	Education, careers
Being healthy	Health, basic care	Health, development
	Identity	
	Emotional warmth	Attachment
	Family and social relationships	Stability
	Stability	Behaviour
	Emotional and behavioural development, guidance and boundaries	
Staying safe	Ensuring safety	Protection
Enjoying and achieving	Stimulation	Education, careers
	Education	
Making a positive contribution	Education, income	Participation
	Self care skills	
	Social presentation	

Figure 8.2 Every Child Matters, Assessment Framework and overview Well-being Measures

What do the Overview studies tell us about how we can enhance well-being?

The quality of care and well-being

Earlier research has shown that the quality of placements varies widely. Some foster placements have an immediate and very positive effect on the quality of life, as well as the longer-term well-being of those young people placed in them. Some children's homes look after young people very well whilst others are marked by bullying, sexual harassment, delinquency and misery. There is strong evidence from other research studies that a key determinant of these differences is the quality of the carers – the foster carers, practitioners, the heads of home and staff groups.[33–35]

The studies in this overview that evaluate outcomes of well-being (as detailed above), or provide a qualitative description of progress, are consistent with these findings. In *The Pursuit of Permanence* (Chapter 2), for example the authors conclude, 'High quality placements are central to children's well-being and the stability of long-term placements for children over 11'. In similar vein, the researchers who carried out *Educating Difficult Adolescents* (Chapter 6) highlight the association between the quality of care young people received, their satisfaction with schooling and their general happiness. The *Reunification* research (Chapter 3) identified, among other predictors of return success, 'highly competent social work' before and during the return. In *Kinship Care* (Chapter 4) placement quality was associated with children being happy and developing well.

But what is good quality care? The composite view of well-being, derived from the outcome measures and descriptive material within the overview studies, identifies seven broad dimensions, as detailed above. And, as detailed in Chapter 6, the researchers who carried out the *Educating Difficult Adolescents* project developed their own instrument, *A Quality of Care Index* (Figure 6.1), which included nine key areas, each divided into sub-categories. The nine areas were: care and control; stability and continuity; safety; inter-professional working; family links; close relationship with a least one adult; ethnicity and culture; friendships; and planning and aftercare. In addition, as discussed above, they researched young people's views of their well-being, including how they saw its association with their quality of care they received. At the practice level, the main areas and sub-categories, identified above, could very usefully inform the dimensions and domains of the *Assessment Framework*.

In *The Pursuit of Permanence* (Chapter 2), social workers identified the qualities they valued in foster and residential care. In foster carers they wanted carers who were: warm, loving, committed and flexible; able to engage with children's families; realistic and clear in their expectations; and able to work with professionals. They also thought that it was important to match children with foster carers. In respect of residential care, social workers emphasised the importance of consistency, the quality of education, the quality of staff and having enough staff.

What is evident from the nine overview studies, including their outcome measures, the case examples and the qualitative material presented, is that a foundation stone of good quality care is good social and psychological parenting. There is a substantial body of literature on parenting, including research, policy and practice material. What is most relevant to the children and young people included in these studies, whether they are living at their family home, in kinship care, or are looked after in foster or residential care, is the research on the outcomes of parenting for children, and in particular, the work on *parenting styles* which underpins the *parenting capacity domain* of the *Assessment Framework*. It is the 'authoritative' parenting approach, combining love, emotional warmth, basic physical care, safety; stability, guidance and boundaries, stimulation, that is most likely to contribute to their all-round well-being. For looked after children and young people, it is the foster carer or residential worker who gives meaning to 'corporate parenting', and as recognised in *Care Matters: Time to Deliver for Children in Care*, 'the quality of care provided has a crucial effect not just on stability of relationships but also on health, well-being and education' (p.11).

The essence of the 'corporate parenting' responsibility is to provide high quality placements. This will require rigorous selection of carers who can meet the diverse needs of the different groups of children and young people who come into care, and who experience different pathways through care, as detailed in the *Permanence* study in Chapter 2. It will also require policies, support services and training, that will equip foster and residential carers with the skills to provide 'authoritative' parenting – predictive of both successful 'ordinary parenting' and 'carer' outcomes – and at the same time not encumber them with unnecessary bureaucratic processes that may undermine their caring role and stigmatise the children and young people they are looking after. Historically, this has been a difficult balance, and at times the 'bureaucratic parent' has frustrated the 'ordinary' parenting that can meet the needs of many vulnerable children and young people. But today we know a lot about what carers, parents and young people want, and how they see the role of the 'corporate parent'.[36, 37]

The ESRC research, discussed above, showed that young people who showed resilience when growing up in disadvantaged families (including poor parents with unskilled jobs, living in rented and overcrowded conditions) were more likely to have:

- experienced a stable and supportive family
- parents who read to them
- parents who showed an interest in their education
- parents who wanted them to continue with their education after the minimum school leaving age
- parents who were interested in their career planning
- parents who took their children out for joint activities
- a father who helped the mother with household chores.

The study showed that a warm relationship with both mother and father was associated with a more secure attachment style in adulthood, which in turn, was associated with greater career success in those without the advantage of higher levels of education.

The challenge is how parents and carers can be assisted and supported to provide high quality care for children and young people. This was the focus of an earlier Overview, *Supporting Parents* (2004) and is central to current Government Guidance to local authorities and children's trusts on the development of a *continuum of support* for parents, as outlined in *Parenting Support* (2006), and new proposals contained within *Aiming High for Children: Supporting Families* (2007). What is envisaged is that local authorities develop a parenting strategy that sets out different levels of support, from preventative and early intervention services through to compulsory engagement with the use of enforcement measures.

There is also evidence from the parents of looked after children that they would welcome more support: to help stop their children going into care; in having a say when their children are in care, particularly in decisions about education, placement, and family contact; and in having support for themselves when their child was in care.[38]

However, whether 'authoritative parenting', is enough for *all* children and young people, is subject to current debate. There is evidence from the Overview studies that practitioners and managers want more 'specialist' or treatment-based approaches in foster and residential care placements for young people, especially for those with emotional and behavioural difficulties, and complex needs, who are unable to be assisted in 'ordinary' placements. A research review of the repetitive and persistent behavioural problems of young people with a clinical diagnosis of 'conduct disorder', suggests that the successful management of severe and entrenched forms of challenging behaviour depends on addressing multiple areas of a young person's life in a co-ordinated way, over a sustained period of time.[39] Multi-systemic therapy, for example, targets multiple causes of severe behaviour problems and may include: parent training; cognitive behavioural therapy for young people; wider family support; and special training and additional support for teachers and other school staff. At the time of writing a national evaluation of 'Multi-dimensional Treatment Foster Care' (MTFC) schemes is being carried out in England, drawing on the international evidence that multi-dimensional treatment foster care can address the treatment needs of this population.

Social work practice and quality services

As detailed in the Overview studies, assisting vulnerable young people and their families means involving a wide range of local partners, including both children's and adult services. For nearly all the children and young people included in the Overview research studies the lead practitioner was their social worker. It was they who had the statutory responsibility to lead on this work. This is not to suggest that they were the only practitioner who assisted them, that certainly wasn't the case. But they occupied a pivotal role in the assessment, planning, intervention and review process, furthering the involvement of other agencies, placement selection and support, and in carrying out direct work with children, young people and their families.

Several of the studies showed that balancing these different roles and responsibilities often proved very demanding, and there is evidence from earlier research that direct work with children and families may suffer in two ways.[40] First, by a shift to a 'case management' approach focusing, in the main on the co-ordination and planning of services, leaving little time for direct work with children, young people and families. Second, by the accompanying dilution of direct social work skills, or what has been seen as the reduction of social casework, using a wide repertoire of skills, to practical counselling. In addition, as highlighted in *Safeguarding Children* (2008), in most areas of England, children and young people had frequent changes of social workers, and the lack of continuity had an adverse effect on the implementation of their care plans. These factors may, in part, account for the wide variation in the quality of social work reported in the Overview studies.

The main features of high quality work described in the Overview studies included practitioners having specialist knowledge and skills, adopting a clear, open and transparent approach, engaging and involving users, carrying out assessments and agreed plans, having the time to carry out direct work, and being supported by good supervision and management. There were also barriers to quality working, in terms of the converse. In nearly all the studies there was evidence of the difficulties social workers and carers experienced in working with, and caring for, teenagers with emotional and behavioural difficulties, and in responding to the problems arising in families where there was drug and alcohol abuse and domestic violence.

Making quality happen

As suggested above, both earlier research findings and the evidence from some of the Overview studies, shows that quality of care can make a positive contribution to the well-being of children and young people, and that direct social work practice plays a pivotal role in this process. The findings from the Overview studies also identify gaps in the levels of provision and inconsistencies in service quality. What will contribute to the development of more consistent quality services for children and families?

Identifying and sustaining quality: a stakeholder model

First, there needs to be a systematic approach to identifying and sustaining quality. The evidence from the Overview studies was that this was not happening in any organised or consistent way. As detailed above, the studies that used outcome measures of well-being and stability showed that social workers, their supervisors and young people can identify differences in the quality of placements. This would suggest there is a lot to be gained from setting up stakeholder quality groups, or the use of existing stakeholder groups, within Children's Services, to identify, sustain and improve the quality of provision. Work in the field of public services, including health and adult social care, has led to the development of a citizen/stakeholder led 'model for service quality'.[41]

This locates stakeholders at the centre of a systematic process – or what *The Pursuit of Permanence* researchers call 'the development of systematic programmes of quality assurance, using the day-to-day experience of children, social workers and key staff' – which include their key role in identifying and defining quality services. This approach will require a programme of research and development into the impact on placement quality and outcomes of the selection, training and support of carers and residential staff. In these ways, the systematic use of this information, should lead to greater efficacy in the quality assurance systems for identifying and sustaining quality services. As descriptive case examples in the public service show, the stakeholder model of quality development also has the potential to avoid a top-down approach, and achieve consistency between strategic, operational and practice levels of quality.

The involvement of children and young people, parents, carers and families, as stakeholders in this process, is central to the development of quality services. As discussed in Chapter 7, and outlined in *Care Matters: Time to Deliver for Children in Care*, and the work of the *What Makes a Difference* Project, there are many good examples of involving children and young people in improving services. The *Leading Improvements for Looked After Children* (LILAC project), initiated by A National Voice, has piloted a quality framework for the involvement of young people in the development of policy and practice, and used this framework to carry out assessment of the quality of Children's Services.[42]

The Overview studies showed that sustaining quality placements had a lot to do with how they are supported. For example, there is clear evidence from the studies that many kinship carers were struggling with children and young people's problems, and that improvements in both practical and personal support would greatly assist them. It was also evident that foster carers and residential staff would have welcomed more skilled help in coping with young people with emotional and behavioural problems, including more multi-agency involvement, in particular of schools and Child and Adolescent Mental Health Services. Several of the Overview studies also showed that a lot of effort went in to the assessment process and finding placements, but then direct work tailed off. The importance of sustaining good quality placements by continuing to work with children and families should receive as much recognition.

Modelling information for quality services

Second, data about children and young people entering and leaving the care system should be modelled to guide policies, service frameworks and the development of quality services for different groups of children and young people. A number of the Overview studies draw attention to the variation in the quality of data collected by councils. But what is also important is how the data is organised and used. Dissemination material developed from *The Pursuit of Permanence* (see Chapter 2, Figure 2.1) describes a four-part working model that will contribute to planning quality services: first, by increasing awareness of the different groups of children and young people who are looked after during the course of a year; second, by showing how they move in and out of care and how and why they move between placements; third, by identifying the type of placements they have; and fourth, by describing what determines the outcomes from these experiences. This approach to modelling will help Children's Services organise data more systematically, in order for them to better plan, and respond to, the needs of different groups of children and young people, and thus enhance the quality of services provided.

Carrying out quality assessment

Third, most of the overview studies raised issues about the assessment process (at the time these studies were carried out, this refers to assessments carried out under the *Assessment Framework*, or assessment, generally). In the seven studies in which assessments were carried out by social workers, it was evident that they were a key process that contributed to the eventual outcome for families, children and young people. As suggested above, good quality assessments are a connecting process between 'the child's welfare' – assisting vulnerable children and young people – in achieving the *Every Child Matters* outcomes. The qualitative material from these studies shows how good quality assessments contributed to appropriate place-ments and interventions, including those enhancing the well-being of children and young people. For example, in *The Pursuit of Permanence* (Chapter 2), the researchers stress the importance of early assessment and planning 'balancing the complexities of safeguarding with a return home', and in the *Reunification* study (Chapter 3), the researchers highlight the contribution of multi-agency assessment to returning children home safely, to better service provision and to positive outcomes.

In the *Reunification* study (Chapter 3), the main components of good quality assessments included: an assessment of whether the problems that led to young people coming into care had been addressed; parenting capacity; contact planning; the motivation of parents and children; the ongoing support needs of all parties; arrangements for education; respite care and contingency planning; whether the assessment process resulted in clear plans and agreements with families; and identi-fying the goals and work required to assist the reunification process, including the contribution of different agencies. The two kinship care studies *Kinship Care* and *Keeping Them in the Family* (Chapter 4), also suggested that the assessment process is critical to selecting and maintaining high quality placements, and identified specific issues relating to the assessment of kinship carers, including recognition of thresholds, the support needs of older children and whether a two-stage assessment process would benefit children and young people.

A number of concerns about assessment were identified in the *Child Protection* study (Chapter 5). This study showed that Government Guidance (*Working Together to Safeguard Children* and the *Assessment Framework*) on the procedures to be followed during the different stages of the child protection process was not always complied with. This included a reluctance to carry out core assessments on complex cases; core assessments not being preceded by initial assessments; and core assessments not being carried out when enquiries were conducted under Section 47 of the Children Act 1989. The researchers suggest that the introduction of the electronic recording system, as a key element of the *Integrated Children's System* should alert practitioners and line managers when agreed processes are not being followed.

Integrated working and quality services

Fourth, the overview studies highlight a number of issues in developing integrated working, a central platform of current policy in Children's Services. For many years, agencies have worked together in response to the range of problems often facing children and families. When I worked as a probation officer in the late 1960s, and then a child care officer, before the introduction of social service departments in 1971, informal discussions and the convening of case conferences with representatives from different agencies was common. Staff from different agencies would also meet up at regular intervals for 'neighbourhood lunches', to discuss wider policy and practice issues involved in working together 'on the patch'.

As detailed in Chapter 5, the statutory framework for inter-agency co-operation was laid down by the Children Act 1989, and, in response to the *Victoria Climbié Inquiry Report*, transformed by the *Every Child Matters* agenda and the Children Act 2004 which established Local Safeguarding Children Boards. Children's Trusts are bringing together services for children, including education, children's social care, health, youth services, youth offending, as well as the third sector. It is their responsibility to ensure that information is shared and that the planning and delivery of services is co-ordinated, although as *Safeguarding Children* (2008) highlights there are considerable variations in the organisational structures and functions, some being fully integrated Children's Services trusts whilst others exist solely for commissioning services.

The same report also recognised that co-operation across agencies is generally good, and as detailed in earlier Overview chapters, there are currently a range of multi-agency partnerships to enable integrated working including Multi-Agency Looked After Children Partnerships, Health Care Partnerships, Multi-Agency Risk Assessment Conferences and Domestic Violence Forums. There is also evidence that the Integrated Children's System, if building on an existing culture of inter-agency working, can contribute to a greater focus on outcomes and a more child-centred approach, as well as a more speedy exchange of information and a better engagement, and awareness of partner agencies' roles and responsibilities.[43]

The research literature on integrated working describes its complexity and captures the challenge on developing integrated teams. It also shows the outcomes of integrated working to be generally mixed. A recent qualitative study of five multi-agency children's teams (MATch project), identified some of the key strategies that these teams used to overcome barriers and to strengthen team cohesion.[44]

First, the research showed that co-location of professionals facilitated team development and made it easier to involve all team members in service planning. Efforts had to be made to involve part-time and seconded staff, and the move from 'co-location to co-participation', was enabled by transparent lines of communication between partner agencies, and sustained preparatory work in clarifying objectives and core roles and responsibilities in the team.

Second, at the inter-professional level, team members with different backgrounds and understandings, or 'explanatory models', need time to explore the impact of changes on professional identities and the implications for service users. The study showed that teams that worked well respected specialist expertise and were able to celebrate the diversity of roles, even if their specialist boundaries shifted. The study highlighted the contribution of effective team leadership in managing this process.

Third, at the daily activity level, the study showed that time was needed for team-building, establishing joint activities and developing shared protocols. The researchers conclude:[45]

> the professionals we worked with in this research are demonstrably seeking to build new ways of working even where they face persistent difficulties. Their expressed pride in membership of their teams formed an important basis for realising effective 'joined-up' practice. (p.198)

Several of the studies contained within the Overview point to the importance of integrated working. The *Reunification* study (Chapter 3) showed that both multi-agency assessment and monitoring was associated with better outcomes for children and young people, in respect of stability after returning home. Also, as regards interventions, the need for a multi-agency approach was identified specifically in relation to: problems of domestic violence or drug and alcohol abuse within families; assisting teenagers with emotional and behavioural problems; helping to reduce placement breakdown for vulnerable young people, by health, education and social care working together, providing additional educational support. Inter-professional working was identified in the *Educating Difficult Adolescents* study as an important dimension of the *Quality of Care Index* (see Chapter 6), and as facilitating effective participation and advocacy work (Chapter 7).

As described in Chapter 5, the *Protection* study identifies seven 'enablers' of inter-agency collaboration: understanding and respecting the roles and responsibilities of other services; good communication, regular contact and meetings; common priorities and trust; joint training; knowing what services are available and who to contact; clear guidelines and procedures for working together; and a low staff turnover. Barriers included the converse of the above, as well as not having clear systems to resolve issues of confidentiality, insufficient resources including time, workloads, costs and staffing, a lack of trust, and negative preconceptions of parents with problem alcohol or drug use.

Policies, procedures, organisational processes and quality services

Fifth, what is the part played by local authority policies, procedures, organisational bodies, teams and resources in contributing to improved outcomes for children, young people and families? Most of the studies discussed in this Overview reveal variations, sometimes, very large, in services, including the use of placements, the availability of workers with specialist skills, as well as access to services. In the *Permanence* study (Chapter 2), for example, disabled children and young people were less likely to have access to foster care placements than non-disabled children, and black and minority ethnic young people had less access to placements matched to their ethnicity. There were also variations in the availability of support foster care schemes (Chapter 3), the use of kinship care (Chapter 4) and advocacy services (Chapter 7). In other words, the direct quality of care, which makes such a difference to the well-being of children and their families, is closely associated with the range and choice of services, and how these are influenced and managed. These are complex processes which, in part, are shaped by national policy, as well as local councils. Having a coherent national framework, including legislation and provision to meet the varied and diverse needs of vulnerable children and young people and their families, as well as integration between national and local services, is essential to the development of quality services.

In this context, the strengths of the *Quality Protects* indicators lay in highlighting key issues, directing managers' attention to actions that might be taken, especially in response to different groups of children and young people and raising questions about practice arising from the performance data. This was seen by the managers in *The Pursuit of Permanence* (Chapter 2) as assisting the local authority in developing as a 'learning organisation'. Organisational cultures are also important to the development of quality services. In the *Participation* and *Advocacy* (Chapter 7) studies, there were recommendations for participation activity and advocacy services to be *embedded* within the culture of organisations, to protect against tokenism, at either an individual or service level. Or, as suggested above, in recognising the implications for three quality levels, strategic, operational and practice.

In *The Pursuit of Permanence* (Chapter 2), the researchers suggest that local authorities and social work teams make a substantial contribution to where children and young people are placed, as distinct from *directly* improving outcomes, which may follow on. On the basis of interviews with managers, they suggest that this is achieved through a combination of policies (e.g. 'threshold guidelines'); central procedures (such as 'signing off' key decisions); organisational bodies (such as adoption and placement panels); and increasing resources (e.g. from independent sector carers through the recruitment of 'local' foster carers).

In the *Child Protection* study (Chapter 5), local authority strategic plans were seen as making a contribution to 'innovative practice'. In one local authority, a domestic violence forum plan provided the framework for the implementation of the multi-agency strategy, the appointment of a children's development worker, the introduction of an awareness raising project in local schools and the publication of articles on domestic violence in the local youth newspaper. There is also evidence that some of the policies at the local level can improve outcomes. For example in the *Kinship Care* study (Chapter 4), the decision taken in some local authorities to approve family and friends carers as foster carers, contributed directly to better outcomes and ongoing support. Conversely, in *Keeping Them in the Family* (Chapter 4), the lack of monitoring of kinship placements by some social workers led to some children and young people remaining in very unsatisfactory placements. Recommendations to overcome this situation include the use of specialist kinship workers, better training, making more use of 'kinship mapping' and the use of family group conferences.

However, the availability of plans, policies and procedures doesn't mean they will be followed. How these documents are prepared and presented, how they are seen to engage staff in their day-to-day practice, how they are customised for different staff groups in different organisations, will contribute to the commitment of staff. In addition, as the researchers in the *Child Protection* study (Chapter 5) comment:

> providing plans, procedures and joint protocols will not in themselves bring about the required changes in practice. Practitioners will need training on the underlying principles and how to implement the procedures and protocols.

Training and workforce reform

Currently, the Children's Workforce Development Council is steering major changes in the children's workforce, including planning for the implementation of the integrated children's service agenda. In April 2008, the DCSF published the Children's Workforce Action Plan, *Building Brighter Futures: Next Steps for the Children's Workforce* covering everyone who works in Children's Services, which aims to strengthen integrated working across all services. The plan identified the rationale for integrated working including the provision of: more comprehensive approaches to prevention; personalised services; shared expectations of all those working with children and young people; better co-ordination and a single point of contact for families; identification of children at risk or harm; and, finally:

> to start to move towards a system where it is the service users, not just the services themselves, who drive design and delivery and where it is children, families and

young people themselves who are empowered to take responsibility for their own outcomes. (para 4.2)

Although none of the studies contained within the Overview focused directly upon workforce issues, most made recommendations in relation to training.

First, following recent Government Guidance, there were suggestions for more inter-agency training. As detailed above, the findings from the MATch research project show that the foundations of effective integrated working requires a shared understanding of different organisations, their cultures, their 'explanatory models', as well as the roles and responsibilities of staff. In this way, inter-professional training can contribute directly to the development of inter-agency networks.

Second, as detailed in the Overview studies, the need for specialist training of staff, including, in particular in the areas of reunification work; kinship care; domestic violence and substance abuse; behavioural, emotional and social difficulties of adolescents; and participation and advocacy work.

Third, using systematic approaches to identifying quality, such as stakeholder quality groups, identified above, to feed directly into the training of carers and staff. This latter grounded approach has the virtue of directly linking the identification of quality by key stakeholders – service users, carers, practitioners and managers – with sustaining and developing quality services.

Conclusion

What has been the legacy of *Quality Protects*? First, as detailed in Chapter 1, against a background of abuse scandals in children's homes, and the evidence of unacceptably poor outcomes for looked after children, and children and young people in need, *Quality Protects* introduced a coherent approach to quality development in Children's Services. On reflection, the comprehensiveness of the programme (Figure 8.1) could be seen as an exemplar of policy and practice development – of how to develop and monitor the implementation of policy – and as such may well have lessons, and implications, for planning future interventions.

Second, the *Quality Protects* programme has raised the profile of quality issues in Children's Services. At the managerial level, this was in part a result of the focus on the QP objectives, as well as the process of involving users and practitioners in project development for the management action plans. But it was also, ironically, a response to some of the complexities arising from performance indicators: for example, whether the stability target may result in a perverse incentive, of young people remaining in poor quality placements. There was also clear evidence that indicators drew managers' attention towards what actions might be taken in relation to the needs of groups of children and young people, not just individual children, and that they stimulated debate and raised questions about services and focused managers' and practitioners' minds. However, what mattered was that the quality issues were being discussed and debated widely, and as suggested above, this contributed to what one senior manager described as his department becoming 'a learning organisation'. Quality was placed firmly on the agenda.

Finally, the findings from the research initiative have been a key component of the *Quality Protects* programme, informing policy and practice. As detailed in Chapter 1, these Overview studies have been carried out against the backcloth of a changing legal, policy and practice context, most significantly, the implementation of the *Every Child Matters* agenda, including the universal outcomes framework and its implications for integrated working. How Children's Services work together, to engage and assist vulnerable children and young people, or those with 'additional needs', to progress towards these universal outcomes, is recognised as a key challenge.

This Overview has attempted to respond to this challenge in two ways: first, by presenting the findings and recommendations from the Overview studies, as well as 'questions for Children's Services', directed at those who have strategic, operational and practice responsibilities; second, by exploring the cross-cutting issues that have wider implications for the development of quality Children's Services. It is the staff who carry out these different roles, who will have a critical part to play in implementing the recommendations of these studies, and, therefore, in making 'quality matter in Children's Services'.

The Researchers' Summaries of their Projects

The following two-sided summaries have been prepared by the researchers and have only been lightly edited. They have been grouped together under the main objectives of the *Quality Protects* programme.

Objective 1: To ensure that children are securely attached to carers capable of providing safe and effective care for the duration of childhood – by ensuring more stability (1.2).

1. *The Pursuit of Permanence: A Study of the English Care System.*

2. *The Reunification of Looked After Children with their Parents: Patterns, Interventions and Outcomes.*

3. *Support Foster Care: Developing a Short-Break Service for Children in Need.*

4. *Kinship Care: Fostering Effective Family and Friends Placements.*

5. *Keeping Them in the Family: Outcomes for Children Placed in Kinship Care Through Care Proceedings.*

Objective 2: To ensure that children are protected from emotional, physical and sexual abuse, and neglect.

6. *Child protection, Domestic Violence and Parental Substance Misuse, Family Experiences and Effective Practice.*

Objective 4: To ensure that children looked after gain maximum life chance benefits from educational opportunities, health care and social care.

7. *Educating Difficult Adolescents: Effective Education for Children in Public Care or with Emotional and Behavioural Difficulties.*

Objective 6: To ensure that children with specific social needs arising out of a disability or a health condition are living in settings where their assessed needs can be met.

Objective 8: To actively involve users and carers in planning services and in tailoring individual packages of care: and to ensure effective mechanisms are in place to handle complaints – by: actively involving children and families in planning and reviewing the services they use, and the decisions which affect them; by ensuring that children in care have trusted people to whom they can speak and who will speak on their behalf to local authorities and others.

8. *Participation of Disabled Children and Young People under Quality Protects.*

9. *Advocacy for Looked After Children and Children in Need.*

1. The Pursuit of Permanence: A Case Study of the English Care System

Ian Sinclair, Claire Baker, Jenny Lee and Ian Gibbs

Aims of the study

This study was carried out in 13 councils in England. It examined three questions:

- What kinds of children are looked after.
- How and why they move into, out of and within the looked after system.
- How far their chances of stability and well-being depend on (a) their own characteristics; (b) the particular placements, social work teams or councils they happen to have.

Research design

The researchers collected data from the council IT systems on all children looked after at any point in an agreed year ($n = 7399$), between 31 May 2003 and 30 June 2004. This sample closely reflected the national picture. There were further data from social workers on those looked after in the last six months of the year ($n = 4647$, response rate 71 per cent) and their team leaders ($n = 114$, response rate 66 per cent) and on foster households ($n = 1585$) and residential units ($n = 315$) used during the year. The analysis first described the children, their careers and movements, and their outcomes. It then related differences in stability and outcome to differences in the children, their placements, and the teams and councils that served them. Telephone interviews with 54 managers provided a managerial context and case studies of 95 children illustrated, deepened and tested the conclusions.

Main findings

GROUPS OF CHILDREN

The care careers and placements of children varied with their age at entry, reasons for entry, behaviour and family characteristics. In these respects there were major differences between *Young entrants* (under the age of 11), *Adolescent graduates* (first admitted under the age of 11 but now older than this and still looked after), *Abused adolescents* and other *Adolescent entrants*. *Children seeking asylum* and children looked after because they were *disabled* also formed distinctive groups.

RETURN HOME AND ADOPTION

Just under half of those who started to be looked after away from home left the care system within a year of arrival. Two-thirds (63 per cent) of those doing so went home, not always successfully. More than half those looked after over the age of 11 had experienced at least one attempt at rehabilitation. The case studies illustrated some good practice in assessing for rehabilitation, but there was also statistical evidence that social workers could underestimate the risks posed by substance abuse and domestic violence in families and the child's own challenging behaviour. *Adoption* was restricted to young entrants first looked after under the age of five. Nine per cent of them were adopted in the study census year as against 23 out of the other 4500 (0.5 per cent).

PERMANENT PLACEMENTS

Among those who had been looked after for a year or more the chance of leaving within the next year was low (around 5 per cent for children aged between 11 and 15). Really long-stay placements were effectively only available to children who entered care under the age of 11. Just over a quarter of the adolescent graduates who were over 17 had placements that had lasted for five years or more, but a third had placements that had lasted for less than a year.

CHILDREN WHO WERE NOT PERMANENTLY PLACED POSED A CHALLENGE

Many adolescent entrants could not go home, could not settle in care, and were not in placements intended to help them with their behaviour. Many severely disabled teenagers were in residential accommodation apparently without the chance to experience foster care in the holidays.

MOVEMENT

In the first two years of a child's care career most placements are meant to end (e.g. they are intended for assessment). After that, around six out of ten placements are for the long-term purpose of 'care and upbringing'. In these, movement reflects the child's age, behaviour, and acceptance of care and, *if the child is over 11*, the quality of the placement. Some younger children stay in placements where they are acutely unhappy.

WELL-BEING

This was strongly related to age, age at entry, experience of failed return, and, *above all and after allowing for these influences, to the study's measures of quality of placement.*

INFLUENCE OF KINDS OF PLACEMENTS

Kin placements were rated as being of lower quality than others but as having more satisfactory outcomes. Councils making more use of kin placements were as successful with them as others, a finding that suggested that this kind of placement could be used more. Out-of-authority residential placements were also seen as being of higher quality, although councils were reluctant to use them.

INFLUENCE OF COUNCILS AND TEAMS

The likelihood of return home and adoption varied by council and social work team in ways not fully explained by the characteristics of the children. So too did the kinds of placement (e.g. residential care or kin care) and legal provisions. Councils that returned relatively high proportions of children home also looked after relatively high proportions of children with 'failed returns'. The children's well-being did *not* vary by council and varied only marginally by social work team.

Messages for policy and practice

Councils may wish to consider:

- Ensuring that their provisions match the variety of children they look after.
- Ensuring that children are not returned home without a clear agreed plan for dealing with their major problems.
- Increasing the use of adoption, perhaps through steps outlined in the study.
- Increasing the use of kin care, whilst taking steps to counter its known difficulties.
- Providing permanent options for 'adolescent graduates'.
- Putting the greatest possible emphasis on quality of placements both in commissioning and in quality assurance.
- Central authorities such as Ofsted may similarly need to focus on the quality of placements rather than on performance indicators which are of interest but dubious accuracy and validity.

2. The Reunification of Looked After Children with their Parents: Patterns, Interventions and Outcomes

Elaine Farmer, Wendy Sturgess and Teresa O'Neill

Aims of the study

The research aimed to investigate the patterns and outcomes of return home, the factors associated with successful returns and children's and parents' experiences of reunification.

Research design

The study employed a prospective design to examine the outcomes of reunification through a two-year follow-up of a consecutive sample of 180 looked after children, aged 0–14, who were all returned home to parent/s between January and December 2001 (excluding children returned within six weeks). The sample was drawn from six local authorities and data collection was by means of an initial case file review, followed by interviews with a sub-sample of 34 parents, 19 children and 22 social workers. At return 30 per cent of the children were under five, 21 per cent 5–10 and half (49 per cent) aged 10–14.

Key findings

PLANNING, ASSESSMENT AND SERVICE PROVISION

The children who were voluntarily accommodated (60 per cent) were significantly older than those who returned on Supervision/Interim/Care Orders. Assessment was linked to service provision and to return stability, but two-fifths of the children returned to a parent without any in-depth assessment. Specialist professionals saw a third of the children and almost half of the parents before children returned and social workers conducted direct work with a fifth of the parents and children. Where no work was provided for any family member (23 per cent), problems tended to persist into the return. A few young people (6 per cent) absconded home or were removed soon after placement by parents dissatisfied with care; children whose initial plan was 'return home' (41 per cent) were mostly accommodated and returned within six months. Younger children with a plan of 'time-limited assessment' (45 per cent) were generally on Care Orders and took twice as long to get home. A few children (8 per cent) returned to their parents, after long in care, because permanence plans had not eventuated.

THE CHILDREN'S PATHWAYS HOME

Whilst improvements in the family situation, or more rarely the child's behaviour, were the primary reason for half of the planned returns, pressures from the parent, child, placement or court accounted for over a quarter. There was preparation for a third of the returns and a third of the children had been consulted about the return. There were significantly fewer return breakdowns when adequate preparation for return had been made and when caregivers worked closely with the parents and/or children to bring about change and remained available after reunification (one-fifth of cases). In practice, in only 26 per cent of the cases had all the problems for the children and their parents been addressed prior to reunion. Often, issues which had the potential to jeopardise the success of the returns, remained unresolved or hidden (especially drug or alcohol problems or relationships with violent partners).

THE RETURNS: HOUSEHOLD COMPOSITION

There were fewer return disruptions when children moved to the other parent (10 per cent) (who generally had fewer problems) or when there was a change in the parent's partner (26 per cent).

SERVICES

Over two-fifths of the parents and children (aged four plus) received specialist services. Families with children on Care or Supervision Orders received the most support. Returns were significantly more stable when specialist help for the parent or child was provided, when reunification work by the social worker was proactive and purposeful and when other services, such as day care, were provided. Support from schools was also seen as important. There were many gaps in the services to support return, most notably insufficient assistance with behaviour management (especially in dealing with behaviourally challenging adolescents) and a lack of help for parents with substance misuse problems. As a result, some parents were caring for very disruptive or emotionally troubled children without any assistance.

THE PROGRESS OF THE RETURNS

Recurrence rates for substance misuse and associated issues (e.g. financial difficulties, social isolation) were high. Almost half of the children (46 per cent) were abused or neglected during the return – half the proportion of children maltreated prior to entering care (91 per cent). Children of substance-misusing parents were at high risk of being abused or neglected (78 per cent); and a few (16 per cent) children remained at home despite ongoing maltreatment. Difficult child behaviours were more likely to recur during the return than be resolved. By the end of the two-year follow-up period, almost half (47 per cent) of the returns had broken down and a third of the ongoing returns appeared to be of poor quality. Many (62 per cent) children were then returned home again and half of these returns also failed. In total, two-thirds (64 per cent) of the children experienced at least one failed return and a third had oscillated in and out of care twice or more. After reunification, a third of the children were not close to either parent and a considerable number said, in interview, that they found things difficult at home, felt sad, confused or angry, yet a third had confided in no-one. They found oscillating between home and care a very negative experience.

FACTORS ASSOCIATED WITH RETURN STABILITY

Return stability was associated with thorough assessment, conditions having been set, addressing all the problems that had led to care, providing adequate preparation for the return and good monitoring of children before and during return. These factors were most in evidence when children returned on Care Orders. Informal support was important, especially for the adolescent returns, whilst parental ambivalence, social isolation or previous failed returns were related to return breakdown. Children over the age of 10 and those with previous difficult behaviour had more return disruptions. Outcomes varied widely by local authority, particularly for the older children.

Implications for policy and practice

1. Returns subject to scrutiny by the courts had high levels of assessment, monitoring and service and were more likely to succeed. A more structured approach to returns for accommodated children and young people and more help with children's behavioural and emotional difficulties are needed.

2. The concerns that led to care had often not been addressed. Assessment and decision-making need to specify what needs to change, by when, before return is possible and how reunification is to be supported and monitored. In particular, more access to treatment for substance-misusing parents is needed and more training for practitioners in working with them.

3. Standards during the return need to be agreed and regularly reviewed, with action being taken if children's quality of life becomes unsatisfactory or if they oscillate between home and care.

Relevance to the Every Child Matters agenda

Given the high recurrence rates of abuse and neglect, challenging child behaviour, parental difficulties and return breakdown, children's safety and well-being during return are far from assured. More proactive practice and greater access to targeted services are needed, backed by clear policy and practice guidelines, with increased clarity about the changes expected, the timescales for these and the consequences and contingency plans for children if they are not achieved. Overall, reunification needs to be given greater priority on the policy agenda.

3. Support Foster Care: Developing a Short-Break Service for Children in Need
Margaret Greenfields and June Statham

Aims of the study

Under Section 20 of the Children Act 1989, local authorities can provide short breaks for children with foster or other families. Most such placements are used to support the families of disabled children. This study was commissioned to find out why local authorities had been slow to develop 'support care' schemes to provide short breaks for non-disabled children, combined with support for their parents, at times of particular difficulty or stress. It aimed to:

*   provide information on the extent of support care schemes and how they operate
*   identify the barriers that might be deterring local authorities from establishing support care schemes, and suggest how they might be overcome
*   examine the motivation and views of carers who provide this service.

Research design

A screening questionnaire was sent to all English local authorities (46 councils responded). Telephone interviews were undertaken with senior managers of Children's Services, scheme coordinators and legal advisers in 14 authorities, selected to include both those with and those without support care schemes or in the process of developing them. Three established schemes were studied in more depth, including focus groups with 20 support carers. The fieldwork was carried out between March and August 2003.

Key findings

No more than a dozen authorities were operating formal support care schemes, although others offered short breaks to a small number of non-disabled children on an *ad hoc* basis. There was definite interest in developing further this kind of support for families, and a Fostering Network project was subsequently funded to help local authorities set up support care schemes.[46]

The schemes included in this study varied considerably in size and scope, but all were able to offer a flexible response depending on families' needs. This was often a weekend break every fortnight or month, but could also involve care in the daytime (for example when children were excluded from school), overnight stays during the week, or short periods of full-time care (for example when a parent needed repeated stays in hospital). Support care was often used alongside other social work support, and was usually offered for no more than six to nine months.

The majority of support care schemes were located within fostering services, but there is a strong case for considering a base within family support services, whilst maintaining strong links with fostering and family placement teams. Whatever the location, support care needs to be presented to families in an accessible, non-stigmatising way.

The most frequently mentioned barrier to developing support care schemes was the priority given to 'mainstream' fostering and a fear of possible competition for resources and potential carers. However, the study found that support carers were usually drawn from a pool of people who would not be available for full-time fostering, or who would otherwise have left the fostering service. Providing opportunities for part-time fostering could actually draw in people who might later move on to offer full-time care.

Another barrier was the lower priority often accorded to preventive services. Many schemes had struggled to keep going financially, and had only been able to develop through tapping into additional sources of funding such as Sure Start or grants provided under the *Choice Protects* initiative. Strong management backing for support care schemes was an important factor in their success.

There was widespread confusion and varying practice with regard to the legal status of children receiving short breaks. Most schemes had decided to operate some form of 'slimmed down' Looking After Children procedures, but were unsure of the legality of this. Since the research was completed, the legal position has been clarified so that the procedures depend on the circumstances in which short breaks are offered.

Support carers were very committed to providing a positive experience for the children placed with them. However, they were generally dissatisfied with the poor pay and increasing pressure on them to accept more challenging children, and many felt that their service was marginalised within social services departments.

Implications for policy and practice

Although there was little 'hard' evidence of effectiveness because of a lack of monitoring or comparative studies, the available evidence suggests that providing short breaks for children in need helps them to remain with their families and may avoid longer-term care. The service is highly valued by parents, and its flexibility is a particular strength. Short breaks can also provide continuity and stability for children when used alongside periods of accommodation. Issues that need attention include strategic planning (ensuring support care is firmly located within the spectrum of services to children and families) and improving support and training for part-time foster carers.

Relevance to the Every Child Matters agenda

Support care is based on working in partnership with parents (or friends and family carers). It can contribute to the ECM outcome of keeping children safe, through providing a break for highly stressed parents, and can help children to enjoy and achieve, through providing leisure and recreational opportunities and help with homework (especially when children go to a support carer regularly after school). This kind of family support service fits well with the ECM emphasis on earlier intervention when problems arise, and on enabling children to remain within their own family and community as far as possible.

4. Kinship Care: Fostering Effective Family and Friends Placements
Elaine Farmer and Sue Moyers

Aims

Given the lack of research on placements with family and friends in the UK (here referred to as 'kin'), this study was undertaken to compare the characteristics, progress and outcomes of children placed with kin carers with those in non-relative foster care and to consider the factors that contribute to success in kin care.

Research design

The research was based on a sample of 270 children from four local authorities in England, half of whom were living with kin (142) and half with unrelated foster carers (128) on a set date, which allowed for a two-year follow-up. Just under half the children in each group were under 10 at this point and most (70 per cent) were on care orders. The children's case files were reviewed and interviews undertaken with a sub-sample of 32 kin carers and a number of social workers, parents and children. The study was carried out between 2001 and 2004.

Characteristics of carers and children

Grandparents were the largest group of kin carers (45 per cent), followed by aunts and uncles (32 per cent) and friends (18 per cent). Kin carers were more often lone carers and were significantly more disadvantaged than unrelated foster carers in terms of their financial situation (when paid it was at lower rates than non-relative carers), health problems and overcrowding. In contrast, the children in the two kinds of placements had remarkably similar backgrounds and behavioural difficulties, although more children in unrelated foster placements were reported to have had past emotional difficulties. Similar levels of parental difficulties (such as mental health, substance misuse problems and domestic violence) had led to children entering care. Children were more often placed with unrelated foster carers than with kin when they had black and minority ethnic backgrounds, multiple health problems or a parent who had been in care as a child.

Making, approving and assessing placements

Most (86 per cent) of the placements with kin were made because relatives or friends came forward to offer to look after children or were already caring for them and were much more rarely initiated by social workers (4 per cent). Assessments were often delayed well beyond the initial six-week period covered by emergency placement regulations. In two-thirds (65 per cent) of the kin placements, carers were assessed when the child was already living with them and some carers felt that the assessment approach used did not fit their circumstances well. If the proposed carers did not meet the standards for approval as foster carers because of their past difficulties or current health problems they were sometimes advised to pursue a residence order; whilst those approved as foster carers were later urged by social workers to apply for residence orders, even when social work assistance was still needed with serious behavioural difficulties or in disputes with the children's parents. Overall, there was considerable variation in how the local authorities used the legal provisions.

During the placements

Kinship care promoted contact but many more kin than unrelated carers experienced difficulties with family members during contact (54 per cent vs. 16 per cent), including threats, assault and harassment, yet contact was rarely supervised by social workers. Nonetheless, the majority of carers (94 per cent) were able to protect children from their parents when necessary. Three-fifths of the children with behavioural and emotional problems in both kinds of care did not get the help they needed. Yet, kin carers rarely had family placement workers, training or access to carer groups (unlike unrelated foster carers) and there were many gaps in provision for the children in their care. Kin carers were considerably more likely to be struggling to cope with the children (45 per cent vs. 30 per cent), exacerbated by problems with the parents, their own health and financial concerns, but were visited less often by social workers than were unrelated carers. Indeed, sometimes the dynamics of the kin families made intervention very difficult. Kin carers made sacrifices and incurred losses to take the children; their marriages sometimes came under severe strain and they could become socially dislocated and isolated.

Progress and duration of the placements

Even though kin carers deal with some extremely disturbed children and had poor support, the quality of the placements was very similar for the two groups, but kin placements lasted longer, principally because there were more planned moves from non-relative care. Disruption rates were similar in the two types of placement (18 per cent vs. 17 per cent) and were higher in kin care when children were over the age of ten at placement. More kin carers demonstrated very high levels of commitment to the children in their care (63 per cent vs. 31 per cent), they were more willing to tolerate difficult behaviour and, even when under strain, they persevered beyond the point at which unrelated foster carers conceded defeat. Placement stability was significantly related to approval of kin as foster carers and to placement with grandparents. Ten per cent of kin placements were clearly detrimental to children and these placements continued for considerably longer than the similarly poor placements (6 per cent) with unrelated foster carers.

Implications for policy and practice

Kin carers require adequate financial assistance to enable them to care for children based on the children's needs and a range of services, especially assistance with children's emotional and behavioural difficulties and with problematic contact and also respite care. A suitable assessment approach for kin carers needs to be developed that considers which supports are needed to enable them to care, without compromising on assessing risk. Thresholds for approving kin carers need to be addressed, since carers who would not have been approved by some foster panels because of poor health, age, accommodation or past offences provided a good standard of care. At the same time, better review and monitoring of kin placements is required so that earlier more decisive action can be taken in those few placements where care is clearly unsatisfactory for children. There may be scope for making more family and friends placements than at present, but it will be very important to ensure that the quality of these placements is maintained. More attention needs to be given to kin care in social work education and in-service training and real challenge to the view that kin carers can or should manage without assistance.

Relevance to the Every Child Matters agenda

Kin placements have a major contribution to make to the *Every Child Matters* outcomes. However, at present children's good outcomes are being bought at a high cost to kin carers themselves who are often under strain. Kin carers' commitment requires reciprocal financial support and services. There is much that authorities could learn from each other about policy and arrangements that facilitate good practice, but such developments are only likely to have an impact if kin care is prioritised at the highest levels within each local authority.

5. Keeping Them in the Family: Outcomes for Children Placed in Kinship Care through Care Proceedings

Joan Hunt, Suzette Waterhouse and Eleanor Lutman

Aims of the study

This project followed up, during 2004–2005, a cohort of 113 children, removed from parental care by the courts because of child protection concerns, and placed with kin. The aim was to assess how far these placements met *Quality Protects* Objective 1 – secure attachment to carers capable of providing safe and effective care for the duration of childhood. The study sought to measure placement stability over time, exploring the reasons for placement endings; to assess welfare outcomes for the children and to identify factors linked with better or poorer outcomes.

Research design

The children were subject to care proceedings ending between 1995 and 2001. There was also a comparison group of 31 children from the same two local authorities, all under five, placed in unrelated care. File data was obtained for all children and for the kinship group only interviews were conducted with carers (37); social workers (24); children (14); and parents (2); and standardised measures of well-being completed by carers (37); teachers (25); and children (12).

Key findings

KINSHIP CARE IS A SAFE AND EFFECTIVE OPTION FOR MANY CHILDREN ALTHOUGH IT DOES NOT WORK FOR ALL

Most placements were continuing or had lasted as long as needed, but 16 per cent were fragile and 28 per cent had ended prematurely. Over half this latter group, though, moved either to a parent or another relative and the carers often retained a positive relationship with them. Only 20 per cent raised major concerns about quality and 24 per cent about the child's relationship with the carer. Almost half the children were doing well and only 20 per cent had difficulties in more than one area of functioning. Seventeen per cent of children, however, did particularly badly. These were typically older, very damaged children who would have struggled in any care situation.

BETTER OR POORER OUTCOMES ARE NOT SOLELY DEPENDENT ON INDIVIDUAL CIRCUMSTANCES AND ASSESSMENT IS CRUCIAL

Eleven factors proved to have a statistically significant association with positive outcomes on one or more measures: the child was young, had few difficulties prior to placement, accepted the placement and did not have to compete with non-sibling children; the carer was single, a grandparent, had provided full-time care previously and had instigated the placement; there had been a pre-placement assessment or a favourable evaluation of parenting capacity in the care proceedings;

and, paradoxically, there had been disagreement about the placement in the proceedings. The age of the child was linked to positive outcomes on four out of the five measures.

KINSHIP CARE FACILITATES THE MAINTENANCE OF FAMILY LINKS AND CONTACT IS USUALLY SAFE BUT DIFFICULT

Children generally retained contact with one parent, with siblings with whom they had previously lived and often with extended family other than their carers. But contact with the other parent and their side of the family was rare. Contact tended to diminish over time, there were often difficulties between the adults and in some cases contact seemed detrimental to the child.

PLACEMENTS WERE NOT ALWAYS ADEQUATELY SUPPORTED AND ASSESSMENTS, THOUGH CRUCIAL, COULD BE UNCOMFORTABLE

Most of the children had experienced multiple adversities and many were showing emotional or behavioural problems at placement. There was evidence of service gaps in many cases, even whilst Social Services were involved, and if difficulties subsequently arose carers did not necessarily know how to ask for help or feel comfortable about doing so. Carers living outside the placing authority were particularly poorly supported. The need for assessment was usually accepted but the process was difficult, not tailored to this form of care and insufficiently future-orientated.

Implications for policy and practice

- Kinship care is a viable option which should be actively promoted. There needs to be an early, systematic and documented exploration of the extended family and training for social workers which addresses values and beliefs.

- A balance has to be struck between the advantages of pre-placement assessment and the avoidance of delay. Viability assessments could precede placement, followed by in-depth exploration and carer preparation using an approach tailored to the unique features of kinship placements, including managing contact. Experienced carers might be brought in to act as mentors.

- Support needs to be improved and could include the contracting out of such work. In closed cases carers should have a named person to contact. Support packages for out of authority carers should be spot-purchased.

- Central government needs to take a lead in formulating a clear policy on kinship care and addressing the pressing issue of financial support. Kinship care needs to take its rightful place, alongside stranger fostering, adoption and residential care, as a major placement option for looked-after children which can also prevent children coming into care and enable them to leave.

Relevance to the Every Child Matters agenda

The Government white paper, *Care Matters*, promises a new framework for family and friends care, requiring the extended family to be considered at an early stage and transparent local policies on support. Kinship care, prioritised in the 1989 Children Act but developing patchily since then, is thus clearly recognised as both relevant to the *Every Child Matters* agenda and requiring greater attention. The findings of this research, whilst linked to QP Objective 1, indicate that kinship care could help to deliver on the slightly different but broadly similar ECM objectives and point to ways in which it could do so more effectively.

6. Child Protection, Domestic Violence and Parental Substance Misuse, Family Experiences and Effective Practice

Hedy Cleaver, Don Nicholson, Sukey Tarr and Deborah Cleaver

Aims of the study

The study examines how Objective 2 of the *Quality Protects* programme *Protection from significant harm* is translated into practice. The focus is children referred to children's social care where there are safeguarding concerns and evidence of domestic violence and/or parental substance misuse.

Research design

Carried out between October 2002 and June 2005 the research took place in six local authorities and involved: a scrutiny of agency plans, procedures and protocols; questionnaires for managers and training officers ($n = 78$); a study of social work case files ($n = 357$); and interviews with parents and relevant professionals ($n = 17$).

Key findings

Although referrals to children's social care came from a variety of sources, police practice in many authorities of automatically notifying children's social care after attending an incidence of domestic violence meant they were responsible for half of them.

The majority of children had unmet developmental needs, lived with parents who were not able to undertake all key parenting tasks, and in an environment which was having a negative impact on them.

Domestic violence or parental substance misuse rarely existed in isolation. Many families experienced a combination of domestic violence, parental alcohol misuse, drug misuse, mental illness and learning disability. When domestic violence and parental substance misuse coexisted the effect on children's lives was more serious.

Plans, procedures, joint protocols and guidance to support inter-agency working were more likely to cover children living with domestic violence than parental substance misuse. This emphasis on domestic violence was also found in local authority training programmes. The extent to which managers and practitioners understood the issues was associated with the training provided by their authority.

Parental satisfaction with the services they received was associated with being able to acknowledge their problems, involvement in the assessment and planning process, and being kept informed. Parents felt the experience would be improved if practitioners paid greater attention to understanding their circumstances and consulting them, and adopted a more honest, open and respectful approach. Half the parents thought planned services failed to address all their problems; effectiveness was hampered by long waiting lists, services ending prematurely, or not being locally available.

The findings suggest that to ensure children are safeguarded and their welfare is promoted requires greater collaboration between children's and adult services. At present adult services for domestic violence, substance misuse and housing are not routinely involved at any stage in the child protection process.

Implications for policy and practice

Children living with domestic violence or parental substance misuse need to be given greater priority in all strategic local authority plans, including those whose primary focus is adults.

Greater priority should be given to providing linked and joint training on domestic violence and substance misuse. Managers need to regularly audit and monitor training to identify gaps, plan future courses and target agencies that are 'hard to engage'.

To address the multiplicity of problems facing these families greater priority needs to given to collaboration and inter-agency working between organisations providing services to meet adult needs (such as domestic violence and substance misuse) and those working primarily with children.

Agreed protocols and procedures are needed to guide practitioners in making professional judgements about what information to share, in what circumstances and for what purposes. Managers need to ensure these are readily available to staff.

To ensure practitioners and managers are aware of local services, managers need to ensure information held on their authority's service directory is comprehensive, up-to-date and easily accessible.

To safeguard children and promote their welfare, services need to work sensitively with families to address both children's needs and parents' difficulties.

Relevance to the Every Child Matters agenda

The CAF provides local authorities with an opportunity to support the police to make more considered judgements and reduce unnecessary police referrals through engaging them in its development and implementation.

The Children Act 2006 and Government's Guidance 2006 *Working Together to Safeguard Children* makes safeguarding children everyone's responsibility and will support adult services to give greater priority to the children of their clients, and support greater consultation and collaboration between children's and adult services.

The establishment of local service directories should provide a valuable resource for identifying and accessing services to support children and families where there is domestic violence or parental substance misuse.

Government Guidance on information sharing (www.ecm.gov.uk/qualitymatters) will help to resolve any issues and disputes between adult and Children's Services. The introduction of Local Safeguarding Children Boards provides the opportunity to ensure business plans, working procedures and training address more comprehensively the impact of domestic violence and parental substance misuse on children.

7. Educating Difficult Adolescents: Effective Education for Children in Public Care or with Emotional and Behavioural Difficulties

David Berridge, Cherilyn Dance, Jennifer Beecham and Sarah Field

Aims of the study

Positive educational experiences are increasingly seen as essential in a rapidly developing society, and for a competitive, skills-based economy. However, many young people looked after by local authorities have unsatisfactory educational experiences and are low achievers. As a response to these concerns, the *Quality Protects* ('*QP*') initiative prioritised educational opportunities for looked after children, and measures of school attendance along with educational attainment became primary performance indicators for Children's Services.

Building on earlier, exploratory research, the current study sought to: investigate the development of policy and practice to meet *QP* education objectives; analyse secondary statistics concerning the educational progress of looked after children; evaluate the educational and wider experiences of comparable samples of 'difficult' adolescents living in foster homes, children's homes and residential special schools for pupils with 'behavioural, emotional and social difficulties' ('BESD'); and analyse the comprehensive costs of care and education services delivered and compare these to outcomes. The study was carried out between 2003 and 2006.

Research design

We worked with three contrasting local authorities and eight residential special schools for children with BESD. Councils' responses to the educational objectives of *Quality Protects* were explored through in-depth interviews with senior managers of both care and education services. We also examined, in detail, the publicly available statistics on educational attendance and performance within these authorities.

The main body of the research entailed a detailed follow-up of a sample of 150 young people aged between 11 and 15 years, and each experienced one of three types of setting: foster care, children's homes or residential special schools for pupils with BESD. They were selected as having presented difficulties in their behaviour at home, school or in the community. Interviews were conducted with social workers/carers and with the young people themselves on two occasions, nine months apart. These focused on young people's school attendance, educational and social experiences, and views about their education and care. Questions concerning young people's service-use and the costs of provision were incorporated in the follow-up interviews. Both quantitative and qualitative analyses were used to explore the data for factors associated with differential outcomes over the nine-month period, as well as the associations between costs, needs and outcomes.

Key findings

A scrutiny of national Key Stage 4 results confirmed that the looked after group performs academically much more poorly than the general school population. However, local statistics can be misleading and are likely to be unreliable. Over the duration of the initiative, authorities received very little *QP* grant linked specifically to its education objectives. But *QP* was accompanied by progress on inter-professional working and general perceptions of the initiative were positive.

In our sample of 150 young people, the fostered, children's homes and the residential BESD groups were quite different: the second had experienced far more adversities. Four in every ten of the sample changed placements during our nine-month follow-up period (between Stages 1 and

2). Changes were linked to the range of behavioural problems indicated at Stage 1, which were greatest for the children's homes group.

It was concluded that young people interviewed at Stage 2 had been provided generally with a good quality of care. There were no differences in the quality of care depending on young people's characteristics, but it did vary by placement: foster homes and residential BESD schools generally offered the highest standards of care. Yet differences in the quality of care did not automatically translate into the degree of progress young people made. The majority of young people showed improvement in a general measure of behavioural, emotional and social difficulties, irrespective of placement. However, using young people's overall perceptions, there was an association between their judgement of the quality of care they received, their satisfaction with schooling and general happiness.

On education specifically, the majority of pupils had special educational needs, mainly BESD. Good study supports were available to pupils across settings, including adult interest and involvement. Nearly half of the total sample changed educational provision in the nine-month follow-up, although it was usually felt that this benefited pupils. The number of school exclusions was reduced during the follow-up, and nearly half the sample were judged to have made educational progress, with a quarter remaining unchanged: this applied across placement categories. We concluded that the QP educational measures were generally successful but changing the official educational outcome indicators is quite a different matter.

The economic component of this study revealed that young people accessed a wide variety of services over the nine-month follow-up. On average (mean), each young person cost £66,300 over the nine months to provide for, some nine-tenths of this going towards placement costs. Dual registered homes/schools and children's home placements were the most expensive, followed by residential BESD schools and foster care. Multiple regression analysis revealed that overall costs were related to young people's needs, measured in terms of the number of problems each had at Stage 1 – the most difficult young people were placed in the more expensive facilities. Hence the paradox that the young people who incur the greatest costs are likely to have the worst outcomes.

Relevance to the Every Child Matters agenda

These research findings are highly relevant to the continuing *Every Child Matters* agenda and its intention to improve outcomes for the most vulnerable children. The educational data applies particularly to the objective to 'enjoy and achieve'. But more generally, the social and emotional experiences of young people living away from home affect their ability to 'be healthy' and 'stay safe'. There is evidence that inter-professional working has improved, as Government intends, between social workers, carers and schools. Furthermore, providing successful, stable placements and delivering a first class education are important targets identified in the White Paper *Care Matters: Time for Change* (2007).

8. Participation of Disabled Children and Young People under Quality Protects.

Anita Franklin and Patricia Sloper

Aims of the study

Increasing children's participation in decisions, both about their own care and about service development, is a key policy priority and a central part of the *Every Child Matters* agenda. Although in general children's participation is increasing, disabled children are less likely to be involved than non-disabled children and it is unclear to what extent children with complex needs or communication impairments are being included. This research investigated the processes and outcomes for disabled children's participation in decision-making within service development and/or tailoring individual packages of care, in order to establish factors which can support and promote disabled children's effective participation. Focus was placed on disabled children who have been identified by service providers as being 'difficult to reach', particularly children with complex health needs and/or communication impairments.

Research design

The research, carried out between 2003 and 2005, comprised: a survey of all social services departments in England to identify the range and nature of disabled children's participation; and case studies of participation activity in six areas to explore in more detail the processes and outcomes of participation. Seventy-six professionals, 24 parent/carers and 21 disabled children, aged five to 18, were interviewed. The majority of children had a learning difficulty and six had communication impairments.

Key findings

- Participation at any level is only happening for a small number of disabled children. These are mainly the children who are the most able to communicate, most articulate and confident.

- Most professionals and parents/carers saw the importance of children's participation, but a broader understanding is needed of the meaning of participation for disabled children, including the importance of children participating at whatever level is appropriate to their ability.

- Participation was fragile and often rested on specific individuals. It was affected by staff turnover and sickness, and key staff having a much wider remit, so that other activities took precedence over participation.

- Most participation activity was not embedded in the culture of organisations and appeared to be carried out in isolation. Disabled children's participation and communication with children, by whatever means suits each child, was not yet an expectation.

- Many social workers reported that they were unsure of the communication methods of children on their case-loads. Even when the method was known, many spoke of not having the skills, knowledge, training and experience for consulting disabled children, particularly for non-verbal communication.

- Preparing disabled children to express their views takes time and an individual approach. It should be recognised that supporting children to participate is time consuming. Where appropriate tools were developed, social workers were given the training and confidence to use the tools and senior management championed the process and monitored practice, participation was achieved, even for 'hard to reach' groups.

- The evaluation of the outcomes of participation activity is still an underdeveloped area, and even though some of the case studies were monitored for nearly two years there was limited evidence of outcomes. None of the case-study areas had systematic procedures for the recording, monitoring or evaluation of the activities undertaken.

- Where participation did happen, all children, parents and social services staff reported positive effects. These included children feeling included in what was happening around them, feeling valued, being listened to, gaining confidence, having attention and lots of fun, and learning new skills.

- However, there were only a few examples of children being given feedback on what was happening as a result of their participation.

Implications for policy and practice

To increase disabled children's participation a number of developments are required:

- Training and skills development for staff, and access to support and methods to facilitate participation.

- Recognition at all levels of policy and practice of the time needed to develop relationships and work effectively with children who have communication impairments and/or complex needs.

- An exploration of who is best placed to communicate with disabled children. Joint working with schools and information sharing on children's preferred communication methods should be part of facilitating participation.

- Participation, whether in individual decisions or in service development, should not be a one-off event. Everyday simple choices are part of the process and such choices can be used, for example, to build up a picture of a child's likes and dislikes when at a respite centre. In addition, information from each child using a service can be collated to inform service development.

- More attention and expectation must be focused on getting the views of disabled children and this should be monitored systematically so that it becomes embedded in organisational cultures.

- Data should be gathered on outcomes of children's participation and feedback on what is happening should be provided to children.

Relevance to the Every Child Matters agenda

Engaging children in decision-making is a key part of the ECM agenda. This study highlights the benefits of this for disabled children but also the need for further staff training and resources so that these children are enabled to participate at levels appropriate to their abilities.

9. Advocacy for Looked After Children and Children in Need

Christine M. Oliver, Abigail Knight and Mano Candappa, Thomas Coram Research Unit

Aims

The overall aims of the study carried out between 2003 and 2005 were to investigate the role of advocacy in facilitating the participation of looked after children, and children in need, in decision-making in the context of attitudes and beliefs about children's capacities at different ages, and according to their mental health status, and level of disability.

Research design

Following a review of the literature, the empirical stage of the research was conducted in two related stages: in stage one, a telephone survey was undertaken of advocacy services for children and young people in England ($n = 75$). In stage two, an in-depth qualitative investigation of a sub-sample of ten advocacy services was conducted. Semi-structured interviews were completed with: 48 children and young people of varying ages, disabilities and ethnic origin; 18 advocates, 40 health and social care professionals; and 13 parents or carers of children and young people.

Key findings

WHAT IS ADVOCACY?

Dominant understandings of advocacy combined elements of representation, support, empowerment and protection of rights. The advocate's role was widely described as 'speaking up' on behalf of children or enabling them to 'have a voice' or 'put their views across'. Ensuring that children were actively listened to and taken into account in decision-making was also a common theme.

ADVOCACY AND RELATED ROLES

Advocacy was commonly distinguished from social work by its focus on representing the child's wishes, and not their 'best interests'. Advocates tended to perceive their role as complementary, rather than in opposition, to that of the social worker, and even as an ally in challenging decisions concerning children's care. Some social care professionals concurred whilst others were overtly critical of advocacy for compromising children's welfare. A clear separation of roles between complaints officers and advocates was identified as necessary to prevent confusion. Most informants felt that involving friends and relatives as advocates for young people was neither advisable nor appropriate.

ACCESS TO ADVOCACY

Eighty-five per cent of advocacy services included in the telephone survey were targeted at looked after children, of which nearly half were targeted at looked after children and children in need. Age groups targeted by advocacy services varied widely in their upper and lower age limits. Young people who contacted advocacy services often had multiple problems that varied in complexity. The most common reasons reported by young people for contacting an advocacy service were (in order): placement issues, child protection, bullying, contact with family and friends, complaints against social workers or residential care staff; problems with housing, welfare benefits and other entitlements; obtaining access to education services; legal problems; health-related issues; and complaints against foster carers.

Advocacy in practice: key issues explored in the report

(a) Independence.

(b) Confidentiality.

(c) Advocacy as child-led.

(d) Children's rights vs. parents' rights.

(e) Children's capacities to engage in decision-making.

(f) Children's welfare and children's rights.

Implications for policy and practice

Findings are relevant to a number of Government policy initiatives, including the *Every Child Matters* agenda and the *Quality Protects* (Department of Health 1998) initiative, which seek to involve children and young people in decision-making and to achieve greater parity between the outcomes for looked after children compared with children living with their families. Recommendations within the report focus on the following elements:

(A) IMPROVING ACCESS TO ADVOCACY SERVICES

Research underlines the importance of improving children's access to advocacy services according to their age, disability and status as looked after or in need by fostering reciprocal arrangements between existing advocacy services; by providing information on advocacy to all children when they enter public care, before reviews, at the initial stages of complaints procedures and before involvement in child protection processes and via the use of diverse media; by promoting good practice between advocacy services; and by the recruitment of a more diverse advocacy workforce. Consideration should be given to the funding of advocacy services on a regional basis, taking into account both generic and specialist provision.

(B) LISTENING TO CHILDREN AND YOUNG PEOPLE

The need for greater receptivity on the part of care providers towards advocacy in particular and, more generally, towards an acknowledgement of the value of listening to children's views and experiences, was highlighted. Individual advocacy is also likely to have the greatest impact on Children's Services where it operates in synergy with broader participation strategies. This might be achieved by using advocacy as a form of internal audit, to collect information on trends in advocacy casework and to enable this information to contribute to strategic policy developments in Children's Services; by including advocacy services in inspections and investigations of Children's Services.

(C) MAKING COMPLAINTS AND SORTING OUT PROBLEMS

The research shows that formal complaints processes are widely perceived by social care professionals and advocates as an inappropriate and ineffective way of resolving concerns raised by young people and that resolving complaints informally and at an earlier stage is generally regarded as a more child-friendly approach. The work of advocacy services should not be diverted towards supporting children through formal complaints procedures at the expense of less formal approaches and wider concerns.

(D) A TRAINED ADVOCACY WORKFORCE

The research identified wide variations in the level of initial and continuing professional development. Consequently, a need for the wider availability of accredited training courses geographically, and targeted at different levels of experience, was identified.

(E) THE ADVOCACY ROLE

Recent Government proposals to extend the availability of advocacy through a revitalising of the independent visitor scheme have met with near universal disapproval (DfES, 2007). The integrity of the advocacy role should be acknowledged and retained. In consultations, most children in public care felt that local authorities should incorporate advocacy as part of their 'pledge' to them.

(F) ADVOCACY AS A RIGHT

Findings also suggest that, to reduce the social exclusion of children in public care and foster their participation in decision-making, looked after children would benefit from having access to advocacy as of right.

(G) DEVELOPING AN ETHICAL FRAMEWORK FOR DECISION-MAKING

Findings suggest that an ethical framework, or set of principles, could be developed with the objective of placing children's involvement in decision-making as a central tenet of professional practice in children's health and social care.

The Advisory
and Implementation
Group (AIG)

Caroline Thomas   AIG Chair, Academic Adviser to DCSF, University of Stirling

Mike Stein   Overview Author, Research Professor, SPRU, University of York, Academic Adviser to DCSF *QP* Research Initiative

Celia Atherton   AIG Joint Lead, and Director, *Research in Practice*

Jo Tunnard   AIG Joint Lead, and Associate, *Research in Practice*

Farrukh Akhtar   Child Care Consultant, Organisation Development and Learning, Haringey Children's Services Department

Steve Barton   Assistant Director, Quality and Performance, Children and Young People's Trust, Brighton and Hove City Council

Lindy Brown   Assistant Director, *Research in Practice*

Sonia Cain   Service Manager, Adoption, Nottingham City Council

Lesley Campbell   National Children's Officer, Mencap

Tony Clamp   Information Sharing Programme Manager, Children and Young People's Services, Durham County Council

Nick Frost   Professor of Social Work (Childhood, Children and Families), Faculty of Health, Leeds Metropolitan University

Jenny Gray   Professional Adviser, Safeguarding Children Policy Unit, DCSF

Jenny Gwilt   Independent Consultant, Looked After Children's Services

David Holmes   Chief Executive, British Association for Adoption and Fostering (BAAF)

Helen Jones   Professional Adviser, Children in Care, DCSF

Janet Lewis   Assistant Director of School Improvement and Standards, Hammersmith and Fulham Children's Services Department (during AIG), currently Head, Turin Grove Secondary School, Enfield

Paul Nixon   Assistant Director, Children and Young People's Service, North Yorkshire Children's Services Department

Hugh Pelham   Executive Director, Children's Services UK, The Adolescent and Children's Trust (TACT)

Martin Pratt   Head of Services to Children, Young People and Families, Northamptonshire County Council (during AIG), currently Deputy Director of Children's Services, Central Bedfordshire Council

June Statham   Professor of Education and Family Support, Thomas Coram Research Unit, Institute of Education, University of London

Judith Stone   Senior Adviser, NSF for Children, Young People and Maternity Services, Care Services Improvement Partnership (CSIP) (during AIG), currently Strategic Adviser Child Health with NHS North East

Jacky Tiotto   Senior National Adviser, Children, Adults and Health Services, Improvement and Development Agency for Local Government (IDeA)

Flo Watson   Research Consultant, CAFCASS

References

1. Chapter 8 provides a summary of the main learning from the Overview studies.
2. Sinclair, I., Baker, C., Lee, J. and Gibbs, I. (2007) *The Pursuit of Permanence: A Study of the English Care System.* London: Jessica Kingsley Publishers.
3. Stein, M. (2004) *What Works for Young People Leaving Care?* Barkingside: Barnardo's.
4. Downes, C. (1992) *Separation Revisited.* Aldershot: Ashgate.
5. Sinclair, I., Baker, C., Wilson, K. and Gibbs, I. (2005) *Foster Children: Where They Go and How They Get On.* London: Jessica Kingsley Publishers.
6. Aldgate, J. (2006) 'Ordinary Children in Extraordinary Circumstances.' In D. Iwananiec (ed.) *The Child's Journey Through Care: Placement Stability, Care Planning and Achieving Permanency.* Chichester: Wiley.
7. Schofield, G. and Beek, M. (2006) *Attachment Handbook for Foster Care and Adoption.* London: BAAF.
8. Rowe, J., Hundelby, M. and Garnett, L. (1989) *Child Care Now: A Survey of Placement Patterns* (Research Series 6). London: British Agencies for Adoption and Fostering.
9. This table is derived from Sinclair *et al. The Pursuit of Permanence* (see note 2 above). It will be included in the dissemination materials being developed by John Simmonds (BAAF) with the authors.
10. Biehal, N. (2006) *Reuniting Looked After Children with their Families: A Review of the Research.* London: National Children's Bureau.
11. Farmer, E., Sturgess, W. and O'Neill, T. (2008) *The Reunification of Looked After Children with their Parents: Patterns, Interventions and Outcomes.* Report to the Department for Children, Schools and Families, University of Bristol.
12. Sinclair, I., Baker, C., Wilson, K. and Gibbs, I. (2005) *Foster Children: Where They Go and How They Get On.* London: Jessica Kingsley Publishers.
13. The Who Cares? Trust (2006) *The Journey Home, How Children's Services Can Support the Reunification of Children with their Families.* London: Who Cares Trust.
14. Brandon, M., Belderson, P., Warren, C., Howe, D., Gardner, R., Dodsworth, J. and Black, J. (2008) *Analysing Child Deaths and Serious Injury Through Abuse and Neglect; What Can We Learn? A Biennial Analysis of Serious Case Reviews 2003–2005.* London: DCSF.
15. Greenfields, M. and Statham, J. (2004) *Support Foster Care: Developing a Short-Break Service for Children in Need.* Understanding Children's Social Care Series, Number 8. London: Institute of Education.
16. Hunt, J. (2008) *Family and Friends Care,* Quality Protects Briefing Paper.
17. *Ibid.*
18. Saunders, H. and Selwyn, J. (2008) 'Supporting informal kinship care.' *Adoption and Fostering 32,* 2, 31–42.
19. Hunt, J., Waterhouse, S. and Lutman, E. (2008) *Keeping Them in the Family: Outcomes for Children Placed in Kinship Care through Care Proceedings.* Available at London: BAAF.
20. Cleaver, H., Unell, I. and Aldgate, J. (1999) *Children's Needs – Parenting Capacity: The Impact of Parental Mental Illness, Problem Alcohol and Drug Use, and Domestic Violence on Children's Behaviour.* London: The Stationery Office.
21. Cleaver, H., Nicholson, D., Tarr, S. and Cleaver, D. (2007) *Child Protection, Domestic Violence and Parental Substance Misuse, Family Experiences and Effective Practice.* London: Jessica Kingsley Publishers.
22. See note 14 above.
23. Biehal, N., Clayden, J., Stein, M. and Wade, J. (1995) *Moving On, Young People and Leaving Care Schemes.* London: HMSO.

24. Melzer, H., Corbin, T., Gatward, R., Goodman, R. and Ford, T. (2003) *The Mental Health of Young People Looked After by Local Authorities in England.* London: National Statistics.

25. Berridge, D., Dance, C., Beecham, J. and Field, S. (2008) *Educating Difficult Adolescents. Effective Education for Children in Public Care or with Emotional and Behavioural Difficulties.* London: Jessica Kingsley Publishers.

26. Arnstein, S. (1969) 'A ladder of citizen participation in the USA.' *Journal of the American Institute of Planners 35*, 40, 216–224.

27. Kirby, P., Lanyon, C., Cronin, K. and Sinclair, R. (2003) *Building a Culture of Participation: Involving Children and Young People in Policy, Service Planning, Delivery and Evaluation.* Research Report. London, Department for Education and Skills.

28. Franklin, A. and Sloper, P. (2005) *Participation of Disabled Children and Young People Under Quality Protects.* Research Report. University of York.

29. Ofsted (2008) *Children's Views on Advocacy. A Report by the Children's Rights Director for England.* London: Ofsted.

30. Oliver, C., Knight, A. and Candappa, M. (2006) *Advocacy for Looked After Children and Children in Need.* Research Report. Thomas Coram Research Unit.

31. Bradshaw, J. and Mayhew, E. (eds) (2005) *The Well-being of Children in the UK.* London: Save the Children and University of York.

32. Schoon, I. and Bartley, M. (2008) 'The role of human capability and resilience.' *The Psychologist 21*, 1, 24–27.

33. Sinclair, I. (2005) *Fostering Now: Messages from Research.* London: Jessica Kingsley Publishers.

34. Sinclair, I. and Gibbs, I. (1998) *Children's Homes: A Study in Diversity.* London: Jessica Kingsley Publishers.

35. Hicks, L., Gibbs, I., Weatherly, H. and Byford, S. (2007) *Managing Children's Homes: Developing Effective Leadership in Small Organisations.* London: Jessica Kingsley Publishers.

36. WMTD (2008) *Making the Difference. Putting the Care Back into Corporate Parenting. A Practical Guide for Local Authorities as Corporate Parents.* London: Rainer.

37. Ofsted (2008) *Parents on Council Care. A Report on Parents' Views by the Children's Rights Director for England.* London: Ofsted.

38. *Ibid.*

39. Joughin, C. and Morley, D. (2007) *Addressing Conduct Disorder in Older Children and Young People: Research Messages for Practice Problems.* Research in Practice Review. Dartington: Research in Practice.

40. Wade, J., Biehal, N., Clayden, J. and Stein, M. (1998) *Going Missing: Young People Absent from Care.* Chichester: Wiley.

41. Gaster, L. and Squires, A. (2003) *Providing Quality in the Public Sector: A Practical Approach to Improving Public Services.* Maidenhead: Open University Press.

42. DCSF (2008) *Care Matters: Time to Deliver for Children in Care, an Implementation Plan.* London: DCSF.

43. Cleaver, H., Walker, S., Scott, J., Cleaver, D., Rose, W., Ward, H. and Pithouse, A. (2008) *The Integrated Children's System: Enhancing Social Work and Inter-Agency Practice.* London: Jessica Kingsley Publishers.

44. Anning, A., Cotrell, D., Frost, N., Green, J. and Robinson, M. (2006) *Developing Multiprofessional Teamwork for Integrated Children's Services.* Maidenhead: Open University Press.

45. Frost, N. and Robinson, M. (2007) 'Joining up Children's Services: safeguarding in multi-disciplinary teams.' *Child Abuse Review 16*, 184–199.

46. Padbury, P. and Priestman, C. (2007) *Support Care: The Preventative Face of Foster Care.* London: Fostering Network.

Index